WALKING

THE

PROPHETIC

JOURNEY

Eucharistic Liturgies

for

21st Century Small Faith Communities

BY MARY BEBEN & BRIDGET MARY MEEHAN

Walking The Prophetic Journey

Published by WovenWord Press, Boulder, CO 1998
ISBN 0-9658137-8-9
Library of Congress Catalog Card Number 98-060910
Printed in the U.S.A.

To order a copy of this book, send check or money order
($12.00 + $3.00 postage) to:

Mary Beben
4315 Runabout Lane
Fairfax, VA 22030

or

Bridget Mary Meehan
5856 Glen Forest Drive
Falls Church, VA 22041

You may reach Mary via email at: mbeben@hotmail.com

Bridget may be reached at: sofiabmm@aol.com

Table of Contents:

Introduction

Jesus told the woman of Samaria (John 4:24) that God is spirit, and reminded her that those who worship God must worship in spirit and truth. Responding to the prophetic call of the Holy Spirit in our times, Christian communities rooted in Catholic tradition and committed to the gospel message of Christ are dreaming daring dreams and discovering fresh visions.   At this dawning of the 21st century, Catholic worship, centered in the Eucharistic thanks-giving and self-giving of Jesus, is being celebrated in small groups gathered as *agape* in liturgical settings.

Many Catholic Christians find themselves to be pilgrims in exile, walking a desert path as God is leading them out of misogynist and legalistic modes of worship and into the genuine worship of spirit and truth which does not revere power, but respects individuals as sacred, created in the image of God. As we struggle toward genuine expression of our ancient faith, we bring with us on the journey the mysterious and deep joy of knowing ourselves to be the Body of Christ in the continuance of the earthly pilgrimage. The pillar of fire continues to lead us as through all generations, a fire of Holy Spirit burning amidst the people.

In his book *The Future Of Eucharist*, Bernard Cooke observes that a new understanding of the resurrection in the Vatican II church has broadened the church's understanding of "real presence" and helped people to appreciate Christ's dynamic presence in the believing community. According to Cooke, while individuals may have specific functions within the gathered assembly, the entire community performs the eucharistic action (p. 32). If this is so, then the gathered assembly *is* the celebrant of Eucharist. It is the community that "does" the Eucharist, not the presider alone.   A community encamps, wherever it happens to rest for this moment in time, around the Christ Presence that infuses our communion, vivifying our One Body.

Historical scholarship supports this conclusion and goes even farther. Gary Macy, chairperson of the Theology and Religious Studies Department at the University of San Diego, concludes from his research in Middle Ages manuscripts that, in the understanding of the medieval mind, regardless of who spoke the words of consecration - man or woman, ordained or community - the Christ presence became reality in the midst of the assembly. Contrary to the mindset of many contemporary Catholics who think that the way the Church is now was the way it was from the beginning, Dr. Macy observes that the theology of the Middle Ages was very broad in application. It was far less rigid than has usually been imagined and more open to different liturgical practices than we have realized. In other words, people were not declared heretics or thrown into prison for not following the norms. (National Catholic Reporter. Jan. 9, 1998 p.5)

Sheila Durkin Dierks identified 100 gatherings in the United States of women who meet regularly to celebrate Eucharist in each other's homes without a priest. She shares the stories of women doing Eucharist and addresses the questions such a new phenomenon raises in *Women Eucharist*.

Small faith communities are gatherings of spiritual pilgrims from different backgrounds who reflect this profound shift in perception toward Eucharist. As they gather for the sacred meal, they celebrate a vision of faith, share joys and tears, acknowledge a cosmic citizenship as people of God, and model the equal ministry of women and men. They believe, as Paul did, that in the body of Christ there is no Jew, Greek, slave, citizen, male or female. (Gal.3:20). All are welcome at the eucharistic celebrations, not only families, but single parents and children, the divorced and remarried, gays and lesbians, married priests and all those who find themselves on the fringes of the institutional church for whatever reason. From our own experience of such community we offer these prayers which we hope will be helpful in the eucharistic sharing of other small faith communities worshipping in the Catholic tradition.

The worship offered in these prayers of the gathered community reflects the tradition of the Church in that the Body of Christ gives the Body of Christ to the Body of Christ. As we remember, bless and share the sacred meal, Christ becomes uniquely present among us, personally nourishing us in Eucharist. As we experience the presence of the Cosmic Christ in this sacrament, we become more aware that our lives are holy; our lives are blessed and broken in the mystery of God's transforming love. Christ continues to die and rise in our ordinary human experience. God's presence is always with us. Our eucharistic celebrations remind us that we are a community of believers called to be full of love as we bring peace and justice to the world.

We have a deep need to express, in action and words, the immense joy of this

identity we share in Christ. We know that we participate in prayer rooted in the
ancient tradition of Catholicism which, in turn, is rooted in a much more ancient
tradition than itself. Joyfully we explore and are nurtured by those older ways as we
continue to celebrate the rites familiar to us from our youth. We are part of the
continuing dance of Creation with the Creator of the Universe, and we acknowledge
the unfolding of this ever-new cosmic dynamism among us.

   This book contains two communities' celebrations of the sacred which we offer
now to others for their spiritual reflection and shared, eucharistic-centered
gatherings. May it serve as a resource for all inclusive communities who worship
in spirit and truth. The prayers and rituals can easily be adapted to the specific
needs of any group. It is our hope that other pilgrims will experience the blazing
fire of Spirit's outpouring as they enter into the celebration of new life. We truly
believe that in God and in the Christ we live and move and have our being. As we
take our place upon the cosmic altar of Creation, we fulfill Christ's high-priestly
prayer that all may be one. The moment has arrived and the celebration has begun!

Before you begin...

The eucharistic prayers that are presented in these liturgies are designed to be recited in parts by several members or by groups of community members. We believe that the consecratory prayers belong to the entire community and should be vocalized in that spirit, not by a single presider.

The Prayer of Jesus is an inclusive prayer; therefore we recommend beginning the prayer with either: "Our Father and Mother who art...." or with: "Our God, who art..." or with some alternative inclusive form of address for God. Please note that there are several innovative expressions of this traditional prayer in the appendix of this book.

We have deliberately not prescribed many "how-to's" because we encourage as much spontaneity and creativity as possible. It is assumed that the worshipping community will wish to create a beautiful and sacred atmosphere in which to celebrate the eucharistic mystery in a way that is uniquely theirs. There are no rules about preparing the gathering place. Let the inspiration come from the hearts of those who come together and let joy be the hallmark of its expression.

It is our hope that these liturgies will serve as a creative impulse to inspire your own Spirit energies in designing eucharistic celebrations suited to your faith community.

Basic Format for Eucharistic Celebrations *

Introduction of Theme

Opening Song

Greeting of Peace

Opening Prayer

Readings

Homily and Shared Dialogue

Intercessions

Presentation of the Bread And Wine

Eucharistic Prayer

The Prayer of Jesus

Breaking of Bread

Communion

Thanksgiving Prayer after Communion

Final Blessing of Community

Closing Song

* Most of the liturgies included in this book will follow this basic format. However, we have included a few non-Eucharistic celebrations, as well, such as an Ash Wednesday Service, etc.

Liturgy for Advent

Introduction of Theme:
>Let us contemplate the Divine Mystery present among us. Waiting, darkness and light, bringing God to birth are all parts of our Advent journey.

Opening Song:
>"O Come, O Come, Emmanuel"

Greeting of Peace:
>May the grace of Jesus Christ, the love of God and the fellowship of the Holy Spirit be with each of you. Let us offer one another a sign of peace.

Opening Prayer:
>Let us pray. Holy Creator, the day draws near when the glory of your Christ will make radiant the night of the waiting world. May greed not impede us from the joy which fills the hearts of seekers. May we not be blinded to the vision of wisdom which fills the minds of those who find the Christ. We ask this in the name of the One who loves us with an everlasting love. Amen.

Readings:
>Any Advent readings that mention the ministry of John the Baptist.

Homily:
>John the Baptist came out of the desert. He was a powerful prophet because he made a large space in his life for emptiness and desert. He deliberately withdrew from the garbled voices of the priests and official teachers of the time so that he could hear God speak clearly. He cultivated only one thing in his desert and that was his mission. From that careful listening to God came the one who would make the desert bloom - Jesus. It was John's job to recognize and point out Jesus when he came onto the scene.
>
>Jesus was riveted by John's example, astonished at the authority of the man. He had a life- changing experience when he ran into John and asked to be baptized by him. Both men were profoundly affected by one another. They found refreshment in similar ways - by withdrawing into a desert place alone and being watered there by the Spirit of God.

That is what Advent is about - dryness and moisture, fire and water, darkness and light, teaming up to enlighten our inner way. As John needed the desert, we need a large space for night or darkness in our lives, if illumination is to take place in us. We need a physical and mental sacred space - a quiet, still place - where God can plant and nurture the seeds that need to grow in us. Our transformed selves can only grow out of that darkness. It is in our darkness that all new life begins and new energy is to be found. When we begin to see the God in the shadows, real enlightenment can begin.

Shared Dialogue:
The community shares their thoughts on the theme.

Intercessions:
For a deeper coming of Christ in our world, we pray...
(Response is: God, hear us.)

That the people of God may labor together to give birth to a new world where peace and justice flourish, we pray ....

That we may give birth to Christ this day by sharing our material and spiritual gifts with those in need, we pray...

That the sick and suffering (especially mention specific names) may receive the nurturing, healing love of God, we pray...

(Other intentions...)

Presentation of Bread and Wine:
(Hold up bread and wine) Blessed are you, God of all life, through your goodness we have bread, wine, all creation, and our own lives to offer. Through this sacred meal may we become your new creation.

The Eucharistic Prayer
Part One:
We thank you, Creator of fire and water and of all the elements of the universe, for you are also the God who lives within us and you are not

ashamed to be called our God. From the depths of your mysterious darkness you call each of us forth by name into the light of this creation that you are preparing as a temple for your glory. For this purpose you called us into life: that we may experience, with you, the glory of God embodied within the many and united in One.

We thank you for the darkness which heals and refreshes, allowing the seeds of the earth to germinate anew. Lead us into the quiet and rest that belongs to this season of the year so that our souls may be refreshed and our life in your Spirit may germinate itself anew. We thank you for the life that is brought forth even from death and for the special quality of light that has been born from the darkness. Therefore, together with all the living and all whom you have taken back into your embrace, we praise your name, O God, our Mother and Father, whenever we pray with the angels: Holy, holy, holy is our God. The heavens and the earth reflect your Glory. Hosanna in the highest. Blessed is the One who comes in the name of God!

Part Two:
We thank you for the life of Jesus, whom you called and sent to serve us and give us light, to bring freedom and redemption to poor and rich alike, and to be, forever and for all humankind, the image and likeness of your presence and goodness among us. In him we have seen the promise of Emmanuel, when we shall all be filled with the completed presence of God and be ourselves the fulfillment of God-with-us.

We thank you for that One who has fulfilled all that is human and made it possible for us to live our fullest human potential, as well. We thank you because Jesus made himself inseparable from us so that we would see that we are inseparable from God. In remembrance, we continue to do what he did. We thank you that Jesus brought us back the experience of God inside us like flowing wine that gives joy and warmth to the human experience. He taught us that we can feed on God as on earthly bread and experience the unity of many grains made into one loaf.

Part Three:
The night before he was delivered up Jesus took common bread into his hands and, raising his heart and eyes to you, gave thanks and said: Take this

and eat it. This is my body. Do this in remembrance of me.

At the end of the meal, he took a cup filled with wine; again Jesus gave you thanks and said: This is the new covenant of my blood which I shed for you and for all creation so that all may be reconciled again. Every time you do this, do this in memory of me.

The Eucharistic Acclamation:
> **All:** In all that has ever been, Christ has lived; in all that has gone before us, Christ has died; in all that yet shall be, Christ will come again!

Part Four:
> From our hearts, O God, we present this sign of our faith. In these signs of fire and water, darkness and light, may we be enlightened ever more fully and come to enter the mystery of our true life in you. Let the Promised Holy One come, rising like a new star in our hearts and minds to transform our lives according to the plan you have always held for us. We beg you, send your Spirit upon us once again; give a new face to this earth which we call home. May there be wisdom and peace as Emmanuel is born among us.

> **All:** Through Christ and with Christ and in Christ, in the unity of the Holy Spirit, all glory and honor is yours, our God, forever and ever. AMEN.

The Prayer of Jesus (Traditional or see appendix)

Breaking of Bread:
> From the Holy Darkness comes forth the Light of the World. Let us share the Body of Christ with the Body of Christ! Amen.

Communion:
> Meditation hymn: "God With Us" - from album *Lover of Us All* by Dan Schutte, Oregon Catholic Press.

Prayer after Communion:
> Father of Light, may the Body and Blood of your Christ, which we receive in this sacrament, reconcile us always in your love. May we who rejoice in the Holy Mother Darkness live united and at peace in this world until the day of

our divinity dawns in glory. We ask this in the name of the Christ who is in us and with us forever. Amen.

Final Blessing:
May God be with you! (And also with you.) May almighty God bless you: the Creator, the Redeemer, and the Sanctifier.   Amen.

Go in peace to love and serve God and one another.

Closing Song:
"Holy Darkness" - from album *Lover of Us All* by Dan Schutte.

Liturgy for Advent/Christmas

Introduction of Theme:
Birther God comes to us this holy season through the stories of daring prophecies, shining stars, unforgettable dreams, singing angels, seeking magi, and the loving care of Mary and Joseph in a Bethlehem stable. As we contemplate the coming of Jesus long ago, let us birth Christ anew in our world today.

Opening Song:
Advent: "O Come, O Come Emmanuel", (or) "Prepare Ye the Way of the Lord", to melody from *Godspell*
Christmas: "O Come All Ye Faithful"

Greeting of Peace:
O Nurturing God, we celebrate your fruitful womb-love, as we embrace one another with joy.

Opening Prayer:
Birther God, you became human in Jesus and showed us how to live life fully. You know what it means to laugh and cry, to walk and talk, to love and be loved. There is nothing we could experience that you do not understand. We know that your mothering presence is always with us. May we, like Mary, rejoice as we give birth to God within us, and may we give birth to God in everything we say and do. Amen.

Readings:
(Suggestion: use *Inclusive Lectionary Texts* from *Priests for Equality*. Tel: 301-699-0042)
Zephaniah 3: 14-18 or Isaiah 25: 8-9 or Isaiah 40:1-2 or Isaiah 41: 17-18 or any of the Advent/Christmas Readings from the Hebrew scriptures
1 Thessalonians 5: 14-18, 2 Peter 3:8-14 or Galatians 4:4-7 or any reading from Advent/Christmas season
Gospel: Luke 1: 46-55 (Magnificat) or Luke 2: 16-21 (The birth of Jesus) or any gospel from Advent/Christmas season

Homily:
From the depths of God's womb love all of us are born. From the depths of

God's womb love, Mary gave birth to Emmanuel, God-with-us. Mary, the first priest in our tradition, gave us the body and blood of Jesus. The Holy Spirit came upon her and the child she bore was God's Child. Jesus is born of a woman. Mary is the mother of God. Mother God is Mary's mother and our mother. God, the Birther of Life, nurtures us with divine womb-love from all eternity. During the Advent/Christmas season, we focus on the many ways we are birthers of God. We give birth to God within us and to God in everything, we say and do. We give birth to God every time we say a kind word, offer a helping hand, listen to a friend, visit the sick, and comfort the lonely.

Katie and Danny, who are seven and five years old, have been birthers of God for me. They see new life bursting forth from mother earth everywhere. On our walks, they proclaim God's glorious presence in small bugs, red berries, dandelions, tiny fish, birds, squirrels, wiggly worms, sparkling waters and billowy clouds. When I am with them, a tremendous energy for play is born within me. They have shown me how to experience God's delight in my life in a whole new way by looking at everything with awe-filled eyes and by recognizing the grace-laden moments of ordinary life. Christmas, for me, is becoming a year-round celebration of God's birthing new gifts and treasures in my life to share with others.   All I have to do is be open and let it happen as Mary did, and as Katie and Danny have shown me.

Today we are called to give birth to a new form of eucharistic worship in our church. We are discovering that, as the body of Christ, we "make" Eucharist happen. Perhaps it is time to ask ourselves: "Do we believe that Birther God is becoming incarnate today in the believing community in powerful ways?" Let us reflect on some of our miraculous God-birthings.

Shared Dialogue:
The community shares their thoughts on the theme.

Intercessions:
For a deeper coming of Christ in our world, let us pray...
(Response is: Birther God, hear us.)

That we may experience the birthing of God anew in our lives, we pray ...

That people who suffer from destitution and despair may experience the mothering comfort of God in their lives, we pray ...

That the sick and suffering (especially mention specific names) may receive the nurturing, healing love of God, we pray...

That those who have died (especially mention specific names) may rest in God's eternal womb, we pray...

(Other Intentions)

Presentation of the Bread and Wine:
(Hold up bread and wine) Blessed are you, God of all life, through your goodness we have bread, wine, all creation, and our own lives to offer. Through this sacred meal may we become your new creation.

The Eucharistic Prayer:
Part One:
Birther God, you brought forth all creation from your Life-Giving Womb. O Love of the Ages, who was born from Mary's womb, we praise you and leap for joy in your presence.

O Holy One of ancient Israel, you revealed yourself in Mary's womb, in a shining star, in humble shepherds, in a baby wrapped in swaddling clothes. You embrace us with infinite love in every situation and relationship. You dwell in the depths of our hearts.

We invite you this day to set us free, heal us, transform us and empower us as we gather around the table of your love. As we celebrate this sacred mystery in the embrace of the Holy One of birthing, we proclaim your praise:

All: Holy, Holy, Holy, Birther of heaven and earth. All beings are pregnant with your glory. Hosanna in the Highest. Blessed are you who dwell in all things. Hosanna in the Highest.

Part Two:
Praise to you, all-giving God, born of Mary. You are the body and blood of

woman. We glorify you, nurturing God for the dawning of the sacred promise of God's Anointed, fulfilled in Jesus, the Christ.

We celebrate the birth of Jesus, our newborn Emmanuel who came to give us fullness of life. During this holy season we share the bread of freedom and lift the cup of salvation. We invite all, especially those on the fringe of church and society, to join us around this banquet of love.

As Jesus gave birth to the New Covenant, he took bread, gave thanks, broke the bread, and shared it with all those present saying:

All: Take this all of you and eat it. This is my body which will be given up for you.

At the end of the meal Jesus took a cup of wine, blessed you, Birther of Life, shared the cup with all those present saying:

All: Take this all of you and drink from it; this is the cup of my blood, the blood of the new and everlasting covenant; it will be shed for you and for all.

Let us proclaim the sacred presence of our nurturing God:

All: Christ, by your laboring on the cross, and your rising to new life, you have given birth to the new creation.

Part Three:
As we wait with joyful hearts for the fulfillment of your birthing power in our lives, we remember the prophets, martyrs, saints and mystics who have gone before us: Deborah, Isaiah, Mary of Magdala, Peter, Martha, Phoebe, Lydia, Irene, Patrick, Brigit of Kildare, Francis of Assisi, Hildegarde of Bingen, Catherine of Siena, Ignatius Loyola, Teresa of Avila, John of the Cross and all those we remember as heros and heroines in our church who inspire us today (Community names, mentors whom they want to remember, living and dead. This list is only partial. Each community needs to create their own according to custom and culture.)

Open us to the inbreaking of your healing love in every area of our lives creating within us new life. When we feel sorrow, give your comfort. When we are empty, fill us with your fullness. When we are confused, guide us with your wisdom. when we are lost, search for us and bring us home.

Part Four:
Embrace us in our brokenness and help us prepare in love for Christ's birth in our lives. Impregnate the people of God with the power of Spirit-Church. May your Spirit birth a new world of peace and justice. May everyone feel accepted and welcome in our community.

Nurture our families and friends with love and peace (especially those we pray for at this time) Embrace the sick and those who have died (name specific people in need of prayer) in your motherly arms.

May we give birth to the Word Made Flesh in us everyday of our lives. May we give birth to the church of our dreams and hopes. May we give birth to a deep reverence for earth and live in harmony with all creatures in the earth of the new creation.

All: Through Christ, with Christ, in Christ, all praise and glory are yours, Birther God, through the power of the Holy Spirit. Amen.

The Prayer of Jesus: (Traditional or see appendix)

Breaking of Bread:
Let us share the Body of Christ with the Body of Christ! Amen.

Communion:
Sing a favorite Advent or Christmas song such as "Silent Night" or "Away in the Manger" etc.

Prayer after Communion:
Birther of Life, Breast of Compassion, thank you for nourishing us in your sacrament. Make your presence continue to bring birth to your faithful people, through Emmanuel, God-with-us. Amen.

Final Blessing of Community:
May our mothering God bring us to birth in every area of our living. May

Emmanuel, God-with-us, fill us with radiant joy. May we be birthers of hope
in our world, and may God bless us always with divine strength to walk justly
and serve generously all those we encounter. Amen.

Closing Song:
    Advent: "O Come, O Come Emmanuel" or "Prepare Ye the Way of the
Lord" *Godspell*
    Christmas: "Joy to the World"

Liturgy of Water

(for Feast of the Baptism of The Lord; Third Sunday of Lent; Easter Season; Baptismal Celebration Liturgy; Earth or Renewal Themes)

Introduction of Theme:
You are a very special vessel that God has prepared in your own special way to be a gift to all of us! Let us sing our opening hymn as an offering of those gifts back to God.

Opening Song:
"Come To The Water" by the St. Louis Jesuits

Greeting of Peace:
Peaceful Waters, we share the abundant love that flows among us as we embrace each other with open hearts.

Opening Prayer:
Spirit of God, you moved over the waters breathing life, freedom and joy into creation. Fill us, bathe us, drench us with your healing, refreshing love. Make us a life-giving river spilling over and splashing justice, truth and love over all.

Blessing of the Water:
May this water be blessed by Mother Earth who has given it to us, by Father Sky who has rained it down upon us, and by the Spirit of the Living God, whose nature it represents.

Blessing of the People:
May you be blessed and renewed in your baptismal promises to God, yourself, and the People of God! (Sprinkle all, including presider, with blessed water.)

Readings: Matthew 3:13-17 or John 5:42f or Genesis 1:1-2

Homily:

> Create atmosphere by placing a bowl of water or a picture of the ocean, a waterfall, etc., in the background. Begin sharing time by singing a simple centering hymn such as "Waterfall" By Cris Williamson - *Bird Ankles Music* or "Spirit of the Living God, Fall Afresh On Us."

> Homilist leads group in five minutes of silence in which community is invited to experience the Living Water in whatever images, insights, thoughts or feelings emerge. Play some instrumental music or sounds of ocean in background. Invite participants to relax, close their eyes, breathe deeply, and be present to the Living Water. Then invite participants to share a story, incident, example or image from their prayer that has touched them.

> If the theme is on baptism, focus the discussion on the meaning of baptism or the call to live the gospel in our everyday life. You could begin with open-ended statements, such as: I believe God is calling me to... I believe I am beloved of God because... My greatest challenge in living as a Christian today is... Baptism means... When my child/grandchild was baptized, I felt... I understood... I experienced...

Shared Dialogue: The community shares their thoughts on the theme.

Intercessions:

> That we may be faithful to our promises to the People of God, we pray... (Response is: "Hear us, O God!")

> That we may use earth's resourceswisely, we pray...

> That the Spirit of God, like Living Water, would break down resistances and barriers between people and between groups of believers, we pray...

> (Other intentions)

Presentation of the Bread and Wine:

> (Hold up bread and wine) Blessed are you, God of all life, through your goodness we have bread, wine, all creation, and our own lives to offer. Through this sacred meal may we become your new creation.

The Eucharistic Prayer:

Part One:

We praise you, Wellspring of Love, in whom we live and move and have our
being. You have sent Jesus, Sophia's child, the Wisdom of the Ages, to show
us that the heart of religion is worshipping you in spirit and in truth. You
revealed your identity to the Samaritan woman at the well. You continue to
reveal your identity to us today. You embrace every nation, race, creed and
culture as your own.

O Divine Companion, you look at each of us with great tenderness. May we
see ourselves loved by you totally. (Invite people to touch with reverence
their own faces and say softly to themselves a prayer like: "I am the
compassionate face of God" or "God's Spirit dwells within me.")

God of relationships, you reveal yourself in other people. (Invite people to
look with love at the faces in the gathered assembly for a moment or two.)
Holy One, Compassionate One, Gracious One, your glory embraces heaven
and earth. Like sun-drenched waters that sparkle, all human faces reflect
your radiant splendor. You love each of us as if we were the only person in
the world. Blessed is Jesus who comes in the name of Sophia! Hosanna in
the highest.

Part Two:

O surging Ocean of Grace, you energize us with Spirit and passion,
connecting us with all creatures in the depth of your unending love. You
wash us clean of resentment and hostility and scrub away the debris that
pollutes our spirits. We ask you to make us new as you did in the waters of
our baptism. Immerse us in the Love that dances for joy in your presence.
We gather to celebrate our sacred stories as we welcome all people around
this banquet table. We remember Jesus-Sophia who invites us to come and
drink of the waters that will quench our thirst forever.

The night before pouring forth his love for all people, Jesus took bread, broke
it and shared it with his beloved companions, saying:

All: Take this, all of you, and eat it. This is my body which will be given for
your healing.

Then, looking with tender warmth on his friends, Jesus took a cup of wine, praised Sophia, and shared the cup, saying:

All: Take this all of you and drink from it; this is the cup of my blood, the blood that will satisfy the longings of human hearts for all times. It will be poured out for the healing and wholeness of all creation. Remember always you are a reflection of divinity.

Part Three:
Let us proclaim the mystery of our dying and rising in Christ: Jesus-Sophia comforts us in our losses, cries with us in our sorrow, and promises that our innermost beings will flow with rivers of living water, even in the midst of our suffering and pain.

As we share this holy meal, we remember the holy men and women who drank from Wisdom's well and showed us how to live as courageous disciples: the prophet Miriam, King Solomon, the woman at the well, Paul of Tarsus, Prisca and Aquila, Clare and Francis of Assisi, Dorothy Day, Jean Donovan, Dorothy Kazel, Ita Ford, Maura Clark, Oscar Romero and all those companions we cherish and who bless and challenge us on our faith journey.

Part Four:
May the Church be anchored in the still waters of your presence where abundant blessings flow forever. O Holy One who lives in our hearts, we celebrate your radiant image in men and women everywhere. Your creativity flows through our beings. Your joy fills us. Your blessings are the wellspring of grace all around us. Your mercy is fresh, like dew, every morning. Your healing liberates us from all darkness and oppression. Your empowerment bubbles up inside us. For you are the Love that dwells in our depths, the Wisdom of the Ages that speaks through us, the Divine Connection that makes us all one. Amen.

The Prayer of Jesus: (Traditional or see appendix)

Breaking of Bread:
Let us share the Body of Christ with the Body of Christ! Amen.

Communion:

"Let Justice Roll Like A River" - *Gather Comprehensive* - G.I.A. Hymnal or "Healing River" by F. Hellerman and Fran Miakoff, sung by Pete Seeger on *I Can See A New Day*

Prayer After Communion:

O God, thank you for refreshing us in your sacrament. May we experience your life-giving waters welling up within us as we serve others with glad hearts. Amen.

Final Blessing of Community:

May the Spirit who moved over the waters of creation renew the earth. May Jesus Sophia satisfy our thirst for living fully. May the God of play fill our hearts to overflowing this day with our hearts' delights.

Closing Hymn:

"Healing River" by Peter Seeger or "Washerwoman God" (Lyrics by Martha Ann Kirk; sung by Colleen Fulmer on *"Cry of Ramah"* - Loretto Spirituality Network, 725 Calhoun St., Albany, CA 94706. Tel: 510-525-4174

Candlemas Liturgy (Winter)

Feast of Presentation of Jesus in the Temple/ Candlemas Day
February 2

Introduction of Theme:
The theme coincides with the time of the year - light is returning to our world. At the Winter Solstice the Light is re-born and the darkness yields to the returning light. Now, six weeks later, the days are beginning to be noticeably longer; the seeds waiting underground have had time to be warmed by the sun's lengthening influence. We are this much nearer to Spring. The ancient feast of Candlemas honors this knowledge, the seasonal return of light's energy to the earth.

Opening Song:
"God of Day and God of Darkness" or any appropriate hymn

Greeting of Peace:
Forty days ago we celebrated the joyful feast of the birth of Jesus. Today we recall the holy day on which he was presented in the temple. Led by the Spirit, Simeon and Anna came to the temple, recognized Jesus as their Savior, and proclaimed him with joy. United by the Spirit, we now enter the house of God to welcome Christ, as we greet one another.

Opening Prayer:
God our Mother and Father, source of all light, today you revealed to Simeon and Anna your Light of revelation to the nations. Bless these candles and make them holy. **(Here bless the candles, which have been set in a basket or container)** May we who carry them come to the light that shines forever. Grant this through Christ, the Enlightened of the Ages. Amen.

Distribute candles to all. Ask everyone to just keep them for now.

Readings: for the feast of The Presentation

Homily:

The coming of Jesus to be presented to God in the temple is seen by the Church as the glory of God's light returning to fill the temple. This is why the feast is celebrated at this time of year and coincides with the ancient celebration of Candlemas. Temples in the ancient world were ordinarily oriented with their entrance toward the east, making the first rays of the morning sun the first to penetrate the holy place.

How would *we* choose to see this feast? It comes 40 days after the Winter Solstice and we can see that nature is responding to the renewal of warmth and light. God is Light; God is Love. All things respond to this warmth. But the fire of that love is in *our hearts*, too, placed there when the Christ-seed was placed into our humanity. When we celebrate feasts like this and meditate on their meaning, we begin to feel the stirring of that new life awakening inside us. We begin to realize that we have boundless possibility.

What else does this day mean? It began as a feast of Juno Februata in ancient Rome and was a love feast. (Febris = fever, the fever of love.) People burned candles in Rome to honor and to imitate this sacred "fever" in Juno's honor. In Celtic Ireland the 1st of February was sacred to the goddess Brigid, for the same reason. Christian Fathers of the Church decided that the candles must be transformed into a rite of purification from this shameless "fever" of love! They turned the feast of Candlemas into an antidote for its original purpose and wove the story of Mary's purification around the day. Mothers needed to be "churched" after the birth of a child to rid them of the uncleanness acquired (presumably) from the act of conceiving the child. The powerful love goddess, Brigid, was transformed into *St.* Brigid so that the Church could control the way her feasts were celebrated.

Oddly enough, when Jesus came, he came simply as the Fire of Love itself and made no apologies for his ever-burning thirst for love. By now his flame has been with us long enough to have warmed each of our lives. It lives in us as it lived in him and is bringing the seeds of our own lives to their fullness. Love is the glory that is returning to fill our personal temple. It will also fill the temple that is our home where we share our lives with others.

Love came to dwell among us. God said to Solomon of the temple among his people: "Here will I place my feet" - revealing the joy God felt at dwelling among human beings. So today we will honor that flame of Love, take it home with us, give it a place of honor and cherish the gift. The candles will be a visible reminder in your own home that love is the center and the heart of that place.

Shared Dialogue: The community shares their thoughts on the theme.

Intercessions:
That we may awaken to the needs of God's people, especially those who experience rejection, alienation, injustice and poverty, we pray to you, our Creator...
(Response is: God, hear our prayer!)

That we may celebrate the Divine Presence in our relationships, especially in those closest to us, we pray to you, our Creator...

That the sick may be healed, especially (mention names), we pray to you, our Creator...

That the dead may dwell forever in your presence, we pray to you, our Creator...

(Other Intentions)

Presentation of the Bread and Wine:
(Hold up bread and wine) Blessed are you, God of all life, through your goodness we have bread, wine, all creation, and our own lives to offer. Through this sacred meal may we become your new creation.

The Eucharistic Prayer:
Part One:
Great and holy designer of all that is, from everlasting you are God! You have woven the fabric of the universe and spread it before you as the dwelling tent of your glory. You have invited all creation to robe itself in the love poured out from your heart as from a fountain of never-ending abundance. We thank you for the extravagance of your giving, for the endless communion

of your presence among us in all that is. We thank you that throughout history you have called to the human family and instructed us to love one another and to learn from the humblest parts of creation your hidden ways.

All: Holy, holy, holy, God of darkness and of light, wisdom of the heavens and of this gentle earth, you who come to us as matter and as spirit. Blessed are we to whom you are made known!

Part Two:
We honor the ones who have revealed your ways to us until we could recognize them for ourselves. We thank you for the courage and fidelity of all the ones you sent to prepare a path for us to follow - the holy women and men of every age and culture. We especially thank you for Jesus who came to us as Light for our journey. He has filled us with Living Light and we seek to follow his example: we, the Body of Christ, feeding the Body of Christ to the Body of Christ in all our interactions and relationships. In him you revealed the complete mystery of love that is the human family.

On the night before he gave up his life Jesus took bread into his hands and made clear the reason that you had sent him among us.

All: This is my body, he said. Take it and eat of it. Then continue to do this to remember me.

At the end of the meal Jesus took a cup of wine, raised it in thanksgiving to you, and said,

All: This is the new covenant of my blood which I shed for you and all, so that creation may be reconciled again. Every time you do this, do it to remember me.

Part Three:
Now then, let us proclaim the mystery of our faith:
In every creature that has ever breathed, Christ has lived; in every living being that has passed on before us, Christ has died; in everything yet to be, Christ will come again! In our breaking of the bread of earth, Christ is being re-membered!

Part Four:
And so, as we take our places in this moment on the stage of human history,
O God, send your gracious Spirit upon us again. Help us to recognize the
reality of Christ present and risen from death among us. Let us take courage
and find power to exult in our great mystery as people on a journey. Teach us
to live gently and gratefully upon this planet and upon the pathway you have
chosen for us from among the stars.

The Prayer of Jesus: (Traditional or see appendix)

Breaking of Bread:
In this sign we share is the Light of the world. Happy are we who are called
to celebrate Life and Light!   Let us share the Body of Christ with the Body of
Christ! Amen.

Communion:
Meditation: "Light Eternal" by John Michael Talbot or other appropriate
meditation music

Prayer after Communion:
 For Jesus and for sunshine, for light and darkness, for one another and for the
warmth of love and fellowship, we give you thanks.

Final Blessing of Community:
May the blessings of light be upon you, without and within. May your heart
be warm to strangers and friends alike. And may the light shine from you to
the glory of God. May you always have the blessing of love. Amen.

I invite you now to come and light your candle from the candle on the altar.
Please hold them during the closing song.

Closing Song:
"We Are the Light of the World" or "This Little Light Of Mine"

(Now blow out the candles and take them home.)

Ash Wednesday Ritual (Not a Eucharistic Liturgy)

Gather in a circle

Opening Song: "Hosea"

"We gather to renew our covenant with Mother Earth by recalling that we are part of a great spiral called Life and that everyone in this spiral - all parts and all things - give to it and take from it."

Show a container of prepared ashes* and say:
"The process of Life is a process of metabolism. We are consuming at every moment that we are alive. We are also giving of ourselves and being consumed at every moment.

This process is not only physical, but emotional and spiritual, as well. We literally become who we are by incorporating into ourselves parts of others! Our ancestors - parents, grandparents, and generations long forgotten have contributed to our biology, but so have the animals, the plants and the rivers - every thing that has life on the planet.

These parts that have gone into our makeup live on in us; what they leave behind is only the ashes of their lives. We will leave ashes behind when we depart, too, but much of what we are will live on in others. Parts of you are already being incorporated into other beings already, even as we gather."

Thanksgiving: Say:
"We will take a moment now to be thankful to all the creatures and elements as well as to the humans who have been part of our journey, consciously or unconsciously, seen or unseen.

Please take a moment to express your thanks aloud to anyone or anything that you now realize has contributed to your life." (The group speaks spontaneously, not waiting for turns, but speaking as they feel led. They may mention rain, fire, trees, teachers, spiritual guides, pets, - any number of people, wildlife, or things. Allow time for this to develop.)

Then say:

"Now please take a moment, in silence, to thank yourself for your part in this ongoing metabolism of creation. Thank yourself for your willingness to give and to take your part in this exchange." (Allow silence and short amount of time.)

Invitation: Say:

"I would invite you to think now of this much larger Life in which we live, for this is the Life that is known to Sophia. In it each one of us is very special. Each one must spiral into bodily form and then leave it again. Form is only one stop for the soul. And in this great truth I would remind you, through this ancient symbol of ashes: **(Hold them up again)**

"Remember, Child of Earth, that Mother Earth has formed your body out of her own Body to hold the Light of God while you are on this planet. One day you will release this form and return again to her embrace!"

Remembrance: Say:

"Before we place these ashes upon one another , let us bring our personal sorrows and losses to the Great Holy Mother. Whatever your personal sorrow, let us remember to be grateful for the Life it represents, for the joys that were a part of that life. If you can hand it over to Sophia at this time, do so, knowing it is safe with Her and in Her. If it is not time for you to do that yet, She will remain with you in love." (Allow solemn quiet time for this process.)

Distribution of Ashes: Say:

"Now please hold the ashes, one at a time, while someone else traces the mark of the spiral of Life on your forehead. I invite you to form an intention, as this is done, of being in a newer and deeper communion with all of Life. For in this way, we find again all that was lost." (Now each person holds the container for themselves while someone else traces the spiral** on their foreheads and says the prayer over them:)

"Remember that Mother Earth has formed your body to hold the Light of God while you are here. One day your body will return to her embrace. But *you* are Light and unto Light you shall return!" (Have this available on small slip of paper for each person to read.)

Closing:
End by holding hands in a circle and say: "Now let us hold, in ourselves, all those who came before us. Let our ashes be a communion with all the losses borne by us all in a sacred covenant of bringing renewed life and hope to these essences - these *sacred* essences that live in us and through us, now and forever! Amen!"

Closing Song: "Ashes"

*** The ashes can be prepared by burning palms left over from last year's Palm Sunday celebrations.**

**** Another symbol can be substituted, such as a cross, etc. if preferred.**

Lenten Liturgy with a Desert Theme
(appropriate during Lent, especially 3rd Sunday.)

Introduction of Theme:

A circle of chairs has been created, with the altar inside them. Ask everyone to stand outside the circle to begin while presider says:

Our theme today is water in the desert. We'll reflect that these are desert years for the Church - for the People of God. As part of that People, we are still on our journey and the question comes to us, as it did to the Hebrews following Moses: "Is God still with us or not?" As you enter the sacred circle of our community celebration, reflect on this question. We will all explore it more deeply during the homily.

Now, please enter the circle, one at a time. As you do, fully realize that you are symbolically renewing your commitment to the journey of the People of God. As we step inside and take up our journey anew, (name) will bless each of us by sprinkling us with clean water.

A community member sprinkles each, including the presider, with a fragrant branch dipped in water and says "Be refreshed for your journey with the sacred Water of Life."

Opening Song: "Companions on the Journey"

Greeting of Peace:

God, grant us the peace and unity of your dwelling place as we gather in the name of the Christ who left your peace among us. Let us share that peace with one another.

Opening Prayer:

O God, your refreshing water rests upon us, bodies, minds and spirits. In it we have your blessing. It quenches our thirst, gives life to the food we eat, and cleanses us from all of life's contaminations. It is the symbol of our life in you. We are renewed for our journey.

Readings: Exodus 17:3-7 or any appropriate "desert" readings.

Homily:

When you stepped into the circle today, you came into it with a long tradition behind you. You bring many things with you into this assembly, just as the Hebrews brought along all they could from their former lives - as much as they could manage to bring. They brought the flocks that were their livelihood, children that had been born in Egypt or born during the journey, memories of Egypt and memories of ancestors that may have been still in the ancient homeland.

We, too, have much that we carry along on our journey - all we can manage to hold onto. But we have had to leave much behind, as well. Like the Hebrews, we have muttered and mumbled to God about our losses, telling the Holy One who has called us here that we are starving or are in danger of dying of thirst for the spiritual "conveniences" we once knew.

We have memories - often delightful memories - of customs and traditions from our youth or that have been told to us by older relatives. Sometimes we miss the "good old Church!" We also have memories of times of enslavement - situations that meant bondage to our spirits and kept us from growing and worshipping God in the freedom and joy of our birthright. We're glad to have escaped that kind of bondage.

But, one way or another, here we are - in the desert - still journeying, often wondering "Is God really still with us?" The rock that Moses struck in the desert is a sign of Christ, who was wounded so that God's love and mercy could flow out to all the world. And the question becomes: "Does that same Rock still nourish us here today?" The Christ has become enfleshed, embodied in the People of God - the pilgrim Church. Does *that* Rock still nourish us where we are?

I believe that it certainly does. But it is up to us - to each one of us - to bring to the group that which is embodied in each of us. "Church" lives on in each individual as we come together. You have something that you have brought along on this journey that no one else in this congregation has of "Church."

Jesus told the woman at the well that the day would come when people would not worship on her mountain (as the Samaritans were then doing) or in Jerusalem (as the Jews were then doing,) but people would worship in spirit and in truth. And if our God is still with us today, it will be as we learn to worship in spirit and in truth.

Each of us must bring what has become embodied as Church to this experience and must share it with the others. For some this will be through particular actions or ministries and for others it may mean a passionate presence in our midst. I'd like to ask you to focus now, during our shared dialogue, on just what has been stored up in *you.* What are you bringing along on this journey that God has given you to share with all of us?

Shared Dialogue: The community shares their thoughts on the theme.

Intercessions:
> That each of us may experience ourselves as God's dwelling place, we pray...
> (**Response** is: God of all ages, hear us!)
>
> That those bound by hatred, hostility, and violence will be set free, we pray...
>
> That the sick may be healed, especially (mention names), we pray...
>
> That the dead may dwell forever in God's presence, we pray...
>
> (Other Intentions)

The Eucharistic Prayer:
> **Part One:**
> Great and holy Designer of all that is, from everlasting you are God! You have woven the fabric of the universe and spread it before you as the dwelling tent of your glory. You have invited all creation to robe itself in the love poured out from your heart as from a fountain of never-ending abundance.
>
> We thank you for the extravagance of your giving, for the endless communion of your presence among us in all that is. We thank you that throughout

history you have called to the human family and instructed us to love one another and to learn, from the humblest parts of creation, your hidden ways.

All: Holy, holy, holy, God of darkness and of light, wisdom of the heavens and of this gentle earth, you who come to us as matter and as spirit; blessed are we to whom you are made known!

Part Two:
We honor the ones who have revealed your ways to us until we could recognize them for ourselves. We thank you for the courage and fidelity of all the ones you sent to prepare a path for us to follow - the holy women and men of every age and culture.

We especially thank you for Jesus who came to us as bread for our journey. He has become Living Bread and we seek to follow his example: we, the Body of Christ, feeding the Body of Christ to the Body of Christ in all our interactions and relationships. In Christ you revealed the complete mystery of love that is the human family.

Part Three:
On the night before he gave up his life Jesus took bread into his hands and made clear the reason that you had sent him among us.

All: This is my body, he said. Take it and eat of it. Then continue to do this to remember me.

At the end of the meal Jesus took a cup of wine, raised it in thanksgiving to you, and said,

All: This is the new covenant of my blood which I shed for you and all, so that creation may be reconciled again. Every time you do this, do it to remember me.

Now then, let us proclaim the mystery of our faith:
In every creature that has ever breathed, Christ has lived;
in every living being that has passed on before us, Christ has died;

in everything yet to be, Christ will come again!
In our breaking of the bread of earth, Christ is being re-membered!

Part Four:
And so, as we take our places in this moment on the stage of human history,
O God, send your gracious Spirit upon us again. Help us to recognize the
reality of Christ present among us. Let us take courage and find power to
exult in our great mystery as people on a journey. Teach us to live gently and
gratefully upon this planet and upon the pathway you have chosen for us from
among the stars.

The Prayer of Jesus: (traditional or see appendix)

Breaking of Bread:
(Hold up bread and wine) Let us share the Body of Christ with the Body of
Christ! Amen.

Communion: Meditation: "God, Mother of Exiles" by Colleen Fulmer from *Cry
of Ramah*, Loretto Spirituality Network, 725 Calhoun St. Albany, CA 94706
Tel: 510-525-4174

Prayer after Communion:
O God, you have set us on the road to freedom modeled for us by your
servant, the Christ, and have given us companions filled with your life and
your spirit as we make our journey. We thank you for all the blessings of this
good pathway we have chosen. Remain with us for our way is joyous when
you walk with us.

Final Blessing of Community:
May the God of Abraham and Sarah, the Blessed One of Jacob and Rachel,
the Holy One of all the women and men who have traveled before us be with
you and sustain you on your way!

Closing Song:
"Peace is Flowing Like a River" by Carey Landrey or
"God of My Life" by Monica Brown

Liturgy of Light

(appropriate during Lent, Ordinary Time, and special occasions)

Introduction of Theme:
Have a circle of candles in the center of the worship space for each person in the assembly. Invite participants to light a candle and say a prayer that expresses how they are reflections of God's love in the world, e.g. I am a radiant reflection of divine goodness... I am a community- builder... I am a person of peace... I reflect kindness and/or patience when I_____etc. Or the focus could be on how the community /church/ earth/world is light.

Radiant Light, you surround us, heal us, shine through us, and energize us. Brilliant Brightness, illuminate the cosmos that we may see your beauty, goodness and love everywhere. Like Jesus, we are the light of the world reflecting divinity's splendor.

Opening Song:
"City of God," by the St. Louis Jesuits or "This Little Light of Mine" or "Sing A Blessing" by Miriam Therese Winter from *Woman Prayer/Woman Song -* Medical Mission Sisters

Greeting of Peace:
Let us share the Living Light dwelling in our hearts with one another.

Opening Prayer:
Enlightener of the Ages, your belief in us far surpasses our belief in ourselves. May we see ourselves more clearly as you see us. May we hope always in the Love that is always more than enough. May we act courageously, conscious that we can do all things because of your power within us. Like you, may we let our light shine everywhere. Amen.

Readings:
Lent: 1 Samuel 16:1,6-7,10-13; Ephesians 5:8-14; Isaiah 2:4-5
Ord. Time: Jeremiah1:4-5, 17-19; 1 Corinthians12;31-13:13 1 John 1:5-7
Gospel: Lent : John 9: 1-41;   Ordinary Time: Luke 4:16-30,

Special Occasion: Luke 8:16

Homily:

Today's readings focus on Jesus as the light of the world. Like Jesus, we are living lights of God's presence in the world producing goodness and justice. The Enlightener of the Ages sees us as we really are - gifts and wounds - and believes that we can do marvelous things. The Holy One has a vision for our life that far surpasses our wildest hopes or dreams. Each of us is a brilliant reflection of God. But so often we are not conscious of our amazing potential.

Let us take a few minutes to reflect on who we really are! (Use instrumental music in the background) Begin by relaxing, breathing deeply, and gazing at the circle of candles. Focus on one candle. Close your eyes and journey to the depths of your being. See yourself as you are before God. Become aware that God believes in you more than you have ever imagined. Listen to God speak in the silence of your heart. See yourself in the light of God's hopes and dreams for your life. You are radiant... loved.... free.... at peace with others... one with creation. See yourself as a living light of God's love, shining brilliantly. Be aware of your thoughts, feelings, any images, insights, or questions that arise. Slowly and gently, open your eyes and come back to the circle of candles. Take time to share anything you want from your reflection, any insights you have from the readings or your answers to the following questions:

How are you a living light of God?   Name others who are living lights of God for you.

How is this community, the church, Earth, the Cosmos, a light of God?

Shared Dialogue:

The community shares their thoughts on the theme.

Intercessions:

That we may care for the cosmos in which the Holy One is revealed, we pray to you our Creator...
(Response is Hear us, O God!)

That theologians may have courage to respond to the rhythm of truth in spite of condemnation, we pray to you, our Creator...

That we may persevere in working for the fullness of justice in our world, we pray to you, our Creator...

That the sick may be healed, especially (mention names), we pray to you, our Creator...

(Other Intentions...)

Presentation of the Bread and Wine:
> (Hold up bread and wine) Blessed are you, God of all life, through your goodness we have bread, wine, all creation, and our own lives to offer. Through this sacred meal may we become your new creation.

The Eucharistic Prayer:
Part One:
God of Light, you shine everywhere in our universe, warming all creatures with your bright rays. God of the stars, you write our names in the velvety darkness of night. God of sun and moon, you reveal the magnificence of creation all around us. Flowers and trees, mountains and oceans, birds and bugs and all our favorite creatures reflect your glory night and day. We praise you for your brilliance, enlightening our minds and guiding us with insight to make decisions and choose paths that lead to fuller freedom.

Risen Christ, you lead us out of the darkness of sin into the glory of eternal life as we glimpse your infinite love alive in us. How wondrous are your works, too numerous to name! The splendor of your unending light sparkles forever in our hearts. We sing your praises as we say:

All: Holy, Holy, Holy, heaven and earth are covered with your glory. Hallelujah for all that has been, is now, and will be. Blessed is the One who is always faithful.

Part Two:
We glorify you, Source of Brightness, for illuminating the cosmos with your indwelling presence. We praise you for the beautiful colors of the rainbow

painted across the sky as a sign of your faithfulness.   We thank you for sending Jesus, the Light of the World, to shine in our darkness and to show us the way to live in peace and justice with all people.

We remember Jesus, who came to illuminate the shadows of our inner world and to shine the light of truth on the darkness of our outer world. The Light of the Ages challenged us to reach out to another, offer forgiveness to the person who rejects us, free the oppressed and stand in solidarity with the outcasts of society. Jesus calls us to love one another with tender compassion and mercy. We ask now that the power of divine goodness move through our beings and transform us to be channels of healing to the people who come into our lives - our families, friends, co-workers, neighbors, even our enemies. So, Healing Light, shine upon us once again as we recall the banquet of your self-giving love.   We consecrate ourselves to you, giving ourselves totally to you in mind, body and spirit. Pour out your Spirit upon us and make us whole.

Part Three:
The night before Jesus gave up his life for us, he took bread, broke it and shared it with the friends he cherished saying,

All: Take this all of you and eat it; this is my body which will given for you, as a sign of the love I have for you from the dawning of eternity.

Then Jesus took a cup of wine, praised Shekinah, the Light of the heavens that guided the Hebrew people in the desert, and shared the cup saying,

All: Take this all of you and drink from it; this is the cup of my blood, the blood that will nurture your soul; it will be poured out for your liberation. Do this in my memory.

Let us rejoice as we remember that we are the body and the blood of the Risen Christ. God of Light, kindle the fire of your love in our hearts. Enable us to act justly, love tenderly, and walk humbly with you. Risen Sun, you have died that we may no longer be blind. You have risen that we may see with the eyes of faith and you will come again every day to shine hope into the darkness of negativity and sin around us. May our lives glow with

goodness as a candle shines in the darkness. May the leaders of our world
and church, and all those who suffer from hunger, poverty, and discrimination
walk in your radiant splendor. May all who have died rest in your eternal
light.

Part Four:
May the saintly women and men of old, the cloud of witnesses who have
gone before us, accompany us on our journey. They are our soul friends with
whom we bond and whom we cherish. Let us pause now to name these
people who have been an inspiration to us. May their courage, faith and
determination be bright beacons of hope and encouragement to us.

Radiate in our hearts, God of exuberance; blessed are we who are one with
you. May we reflect your holy presence and lifegiving power as we carry
each other out of the darkness of misunderstanding, hatred, and fear into the
wondrous light of understanding, love and trust.

Make us your co-workers in affirming human dignity. Help us to challenge a
culture that seeks to dominate rather than to empower. May we be prophetic
in working for systemic justice, always questioning structures that oppress,
denigrate, and exclude women, homosexuals, foreigners, and all the
contemporary outcasts in our society today. As the prophet Isaiah said, when
we speak truth to power, our wound will be quickly healed. Consecrate us
now in your truth as we pray for a new outpouring of the Spirit in our time:

All: Through Christ, the Light of the World, with Christ, the Light of the
World, in Christ, the Light of the World, all glory, power and honor is yours
Creator of the Universe, through the power of the Spirit that makes us all one
now and ever. Amen.

(Place candles on table and join hands.)

The Prayer of Jesus: (Traditional or see appendix)

Breaking of Bread:
(Hold up bread and wine) Through this sacred meal may we become your
new creation. Let us share the Body of Christ with the Body of Christ!

Communion:

Instrumental Music - Mike Rowland's "The Fairy Ring" or any song from John Michael Talbot's *The God of Life.* or "Jesus, Wonderful Counselor" (*Praise Six* by the Maranatha Singers)

Prayer after Communion:

Thank you, God, for the meal we have shared in your memory. May we go forth from here as a light of your love, more deeply aware of our communion with God and all creatures. Through the power of your Spirit, we pray. Amen.

Final Blessing of Community:

May the love of God enfold us; may the light of God brighten our paths; may the Spirit of God dance within our hearts as we go from glory to glory on our pilgrimage to eternity's shore.

Closing Song:

"Come to the Circle" by Kathy Sherman in *Once Upon a Universe* published by Sisters of St. Joseph, La Grange, Illinois 1-800-354-3504. or " Send us Forth, O Christ Sophia" by Jann Aldredge-Clanton, published by Twenty-Third Publications 1-800-321-0411.

A New Liturgy For An Easter Vigil Service

(This ends with a Eucharistic Liturgy. In this service, we try to give as many people as possible a part to play.)

In a room with a fireplace, light and bless the new fire:
> God of the Universe, we share in the light of your glory through the Christ living in this community that you have formed. Make this new fire holy and inflame us with new hope. Purify our minds by this celebration and enkindle in us your holy wisdom. Amen.

Bless the new water:
> God, our Mother and Father, this night your people keep prayerful vigil. Be with us as we recall the wonder of our creation. Bless this water; it makes the seeds grow; it refreshes us and makes us clean. You have made of it a servant of your loving kindness. Through water you set your people free and quenched their thirst in the desert. With water the prophets announced a new covenant that you would make with humanity. Let this water remind us of our baptism and of our covenant with all the earth. Amen.

(Everyone sit down around fire on pillows, floor, or chairs.)

Introduction:
> Dear friends in Christ, we have begun our solemn vigil. Let us recall how we have been called throughout all of history as God has led us in all our generations. And, through this celebration, may God bring to perfection the saving work begun in us. Amen.
>
> Tonight we will tell stories around this fire to remember how our ancestors lived and to recall the events which have made us into a people of God.

(Note: These stories are not read, but *told* as a true storyteller would do!)

1. **The Story of Creation**   (After this story, a cantor sings:) "I have loved you with an everlasting love; I have called you and you are mine."
All sing: "I have loved you with an everlasting love; I have loved you and you are mine!"

2. **The Story of Abraham and Sarah**   (Cantor sings: "I have loved you...etc." All sing the response.)

3. **The Story of Aaron, Miriam, and Moses and the First Passover** (Cantor sings, etc. as above)

(As many other Old Testament stories may be added as the community wishes, keeping in mind that the entire service takes a bit of time.)

Now a community member, preferably a man, lights a taper from the fire and from that lights an earthenware candle to carry into the dining room. (This symbolizes the continuity of the One Light.) Another member, preferably a woman, carries a pitcher of water, symbolizing the Living Water. A child, or the youngest member, walks with them and carries the "story" (the Bible). They walk at the head of the people who follow them on this symbolic journey - into the dining area. (Note: This is an important metaphor for the way the people of God *actually* carry these myths forward in time.)

Cantor sings as we move in procession (as a people of God) into dining area for the Seder supper: "I have loved you...etc." and people respond, as before.

The candle and water are placed, with the book between them, on a small table in dining area that has been arranged so all can see.

The candles for the meal are lighted as the blessing is said:
Blessed are you, Ruler of the Universe! You have blessed us and directed us to kindle the holy day light! Blessed are you, our God! You have given us

life, kept us safely, and brought us to this holy season!

Pour the first cup of wine.
Raise the first cup of wine while leader of Seder says:
Blessed are you, Ruler of the Universe, Creator of the fruit of the vine!
Blessed are you, Who has chosen us and blessed us with the commandments.
Out of love you gave us festivals for happiness, holy days and seasons of joy,
this Passover season, our festival of freedom! This holy assembly is called
together in love to remember the Exodus from Egypt.

All drink the first cup of wine.

Someone pours water over leader's fingers from the pitcher while leader
washes hands and recites: Blessed are you, Ruler of the Universe! You
have blessed us with the commandments and directed us to have clean
hands.

Leader holds up a sprig of parsley; all do the same. Leader says:
Blessed are you, our God, Creator of the produce of the earth! (All dip the
parsley into salt water and eat it.)

Leader uncovers dish of matzo; holds one up for all to see and says:
See the bread of affliction which our ancestors ate in Egypt. All you who
are hungry, come eat with us! This year we are here. May next year find us
celebrating the Passover in Jerusalem! This year men and women are
enslaved; may next year see them free!

Divide this matzo among those present and eat it.

Cover matzos again; refill wine glasses the second time (do not drink yet!)

The Four Questions:
Tradition is preserved for future generations by having our children take part
in our rituals and celebrations. The youngest present is required to ask four
important questions.

The Leader says:

This night is very different from all other nights! (cue for the questions to
be asked)

Youngest Present:

1.On all other nights we may eat bread or matzo. Why on this night may we
eat only matzo?
2.On all other nights we may eat any kind of salad greens. Why on this night
must we taste bitter greens?
3.On all other nights we don't need to dip any food into another. Why on this
night must we dip the parsley into salt water and the bitter herb into charoses?
4.On all other nights we may eat sitting upright or at ease. Why on this night
must we all be at ease?

Leader uncovers the matzos again and says:

We celebrate tonight because we were Pharaoh's slaves in Egypt, but God
rescued us with a mighty hand and an outstretched arm. We are all at ease to
show that we are free people. We eat matzo tonight to remember the bread
our ancestors ate in the desert after the exodus and we eat bitter greens to
remember their affliction under the cruel taskmasters of Egypt. We dip the
good green herbs into salt water to remember the tears of those times, even as
we enjoy the bounty of the earth, and also to recall the sprig of hyssop with
which our ancestors sprinkled blood on their doorposts to mark their houses
so the angel of death would pass over them. The charoses, made from apples,
wine and honey reminds us of the mixture of mud and straw which our
ancestors had to use to bake bricks for the Egyptians. We eat this with bitter
herbs to acknowledge that even in such bitter times there is some sweetness.

If God had not brought our forefathers and mothers out of Egypt, then we and
our children and our children's children might still be enslaved to Pharaoh in
Egypt. Therefore, even if all of us were women and men of learning and
understanding, ripe in age and wisdom and well-versed in the Torah, it would
still be our duty each year to repeat the story of the exodus from Egypt. And
the man or woman who enjoys elaborating on the story of that liberation is to
be admired.

We now recount the ten plagues which God visited on the Egyptians. As we name each plague, each of us must let drop from his or her finger a drop of wine from our cup. This is done to remind us that it was through the pain of human beings, even though they may have been enemies, that we have enjoyed our freedom. Suffering and pain among our fellow humans, whoever they are, is always a loss from the wine of joy in the cup of life.

Drop wine onto plate as each word is said:
Blood - Frogs - Lice - Flies - Disease of Cattle - Boils - Hail - Locusts - Darkness - Death of every first-born male among animals and humans

Leader:
In every generation it is each person's duty to look upon one's self as if she or he personally came out of Egypt.

Take the top matzo; break and distribute to all. Place horseradish and charoses on small piece and eat it. All do the same.

All raise wine cups and recite:
Therefore it is our duty ever to thank, praise, glorify, bless and adore God who accomplished all these wonders for our parents and us. God led us from bondage to freedom, from sorrow to joy, from mourning to celebration, from deep darkness to great light, from enslavement to emancipation. Let us sing anew unto God. Blessed are you, Ruler of the Universe, Creator of the fruit of the vine!

Drink the second cup of wine

Eat the Passover Meal

When all are nearly finished, read: Isaiah 55 (or any appropriate scripture)

Refill the wine cups; all raise the third cup of wine and recite:
Blessed are you, our God, who creates the fruit of the vine!
All drink the third cup

Leader:

It was at this point in the Supper that Jesus took the bread and wine and gave them a new meaning for his friends and disciples, saying "Take these and eat, for this is my body which shall be given up for you! Do this is remembrance of me!" We shall now, then, continue our journey as the people of God, into the Eucharistic era.

Read Romans 6: 3-11 Say:

In Jesus the Old Covenant came to its perfection and continued into the New Covenant where the people of God diversified into those who celebrated the new way and those who continued to cherish the old. Both groups continue, even today, to commemorate the action of God in our history, gathering around the Passover table or the table of the Eucharist, keeping the commandment to celebrate this holy event in all our generations.

We have now come to another moment in history when we are moving on another step of this one great journey. To represent this movement, we will now move into the living room*, still in procession as the people of God, taking with us the fire and the water, along with the story. All of these have been with us since desert times and we have blessed them anew this night. As a people, these symbols are our sacred heritage and we must hand them on to generations to come after us! Let us move, symbolically, into the new land that God is opening up before us where we will now celebrate our Eucharist. (Carry fire, water, and book into the prepared room and light Christ candle from the earthenware candle, *without extinguishing the former candle.*)

Cantor:

Sing the "Exultet," with people responding.

Read the gospel - Luke 24: 1-12

Group share the homily:

Some thoughts about the continuity of our faith journey and our on-going responsibility for the passing on of this faith to future generations would be appropriate. Make clear that this is an historic and prophetic task and moment and despite our possible alienation from the institutional mode, we must walk it.

Intercessions:
That we may learn to be a faithful people, we pray...
(**Response** is: God of all ages, hear our prayer!)

That we the pillar of fire may burn within our hearts as a guide, we pray...

That we may welcome all who wish to join us, whether friend or stranger, especially the most needful of God's compassion, we pray...

That we may be a witness to the Living God, resurrected in us, we pray...

(Other Intentions)

Presentation of the Bread and Wine:
(Hold up bread and wine) Blessed are you, God of all life, through your goodness we have bread, wine, all creation, and our own lives to offer. Through this sacred meal may we become your new creation.

The Eucharistic Prayer:
Part One:
Great and holy Designer of all that is, from everlasting you are God! You have woven the fabric of the universe and spread it before you as the dwelling tent of your glory. You have invited all creation to robe itself in the love poured out from your heart as from a fountain of never-ending abundance.

We thank you for the extravagance of your giving, for the endless communion of your presence among us in all that is. We thank you that throughout history you have called to the human family and instructed us to love one another and to learn, from the humblest parts of creation, your hidden ways.

On this holiest of nights, when you called us out of slavery forever through the life of the Christ, renew our solemn relationship of everlasting love with you and remind us of the covenant you have made with us for all time.

All: Holy, holy, holy, God of darkness and of light, wisdom of the heavens and of this gentle earth, you who come to us as matter and as spirit; blessed are we to whom you are made known!

Part Two:
We honor the ones who have revealed your ways to us until we could recognize them for ourselves. We thank you for the courage and fidelity of all the ones you sent to prepare a path for us to follow - the holy women and men of every age and culture.

We especially thank you for Jesus who came to us as bread for our journey. He has become Living Bread and we seek to follow his example: we, the Body of Christ, feeding the Body of Christ to the Body of Christ in all our interactions and relationships. In Christ you revealed the complete mystery of love that is the human family.

On the night before he gave up his life Jesus took bread into his hands and made clear the reason that you had sent him among us.

All: This is my body, he said. Take it and eat of it. Then continue to do this to remember me. **(Use the last matzo for this consecration.)**

At the end of the meal Jesus took a cup of wine, raised it in thanksgiving to you, and said,

All: This is the new covenant of my blood which I shed for you and all, so that creation may be reconciled again. Every time you do this, do it to remember me. **(Consecrate the last cup of wine.)**

Part Three:
Now then, let us proclaim the mystery of our faith:
In every creature that has ever breathed, Christ has lived;

in every living being that has passed on before us, Christ has died;
in everything yet to be, Christ will come again!
In our breaking of the bread of earth, Christ is being re-membered!

Part Four:
And so, as we take our places in this moment on the stage of human history,
O God, send your gracious Spirit upon us again. Help us to recognize the
reality of Christ present among us. Let us take courage and find power to
exult in our great mystery as people on a journey. Teach us to live gently and
gratefully upon this planet and upon the pathway you have chosen for us from
among the stars.

Breaking of Bread:
This is our Living Passover Sacrifice; Blessed are we who are called to this
Supper! Let us share the Body of Christ with the Body of Christ! Amen.

Communion:
Meditation Music or Easter Hymn or "Move With One Heart" by *The Monks
of Western Priory*

Final Blessing of Community:
God has called you in all your generations to be a royal priesthood, a holy
nation, a people known for Love. Go now to carry this love to all you meet!

Closing Hymn -
"Let All The Earth" (*Glory and Praise 2*) or any Easter hymn that is
appropriate.

Share Coffee and Dessert!

* This can be any room that has been prepared ahead of time with flowers, Easter
theme, and a Christ candle.

Liturgy on The Cosmic Dance

(Spring or Summer)

Introduction of Theme:
Our Creator calls us to join the cosmic dance of creation - women, men, children, all creatures - leaping, spinning, twirling through time and space in a celebration of praise that echoes throughout the universe forever. Let us put on our dancing shoes and feel the divine energy of Spirit-Life moving among us, around us, within us - everywhere we turn.

Opening Song:
"Circle of Love" by Miriam Therese Winter

Greeting of Peace:
(Music: Instrumental music. Group forms a circle and move three steps to the right and then one step to the left as the music plays. Other steps could be designed by liturgical planners in response to the culture and creativity of the community.)
 Let us join hands in a circle and move to the right and to the left at the beat of the music. As we do so, let us experience the energy of the divine dance connecting us in love with all creation. Let our circle dance express our deep desire for peace and harmony in the cosmos.

(Alternate Greeting:) Let us join hands in a circle as a sign of our solidarity with all creation.

Opening Prayer:
In the name of our God who dwells within us, in the name of our God, who is bearer of earth's magnificent gifts: daffodils and oak trees, sparkling oceans, and majestic mountains, strong bears and tiny kittens, in the name of our God who dances on moon beams, and leaps for joy across the heavens, let us give thanks and praise.

Readings:
Genesis 1:1-27;   Gospel: John 14:11-21

Homily:
As we listen to the affirmation of the Creator, proclaiming the creation to be good in the Genesis story of creation, we receive a divine invitation to dance forever with the Divine Mystery that is sometimes hidden, sometimes unveiled in everyone and everything we encounter.

Seven-year-old Katie and five-year-old Danny have shown me how glorious is dancing with the Holy One. Sometimes it means putting on shoes and jumping in puddles, or dining with princes and princesses, or running barefoot through the grass, or imitating mother eagle teaching her baby eaglets how to fly, or playing and splashing in a swimming pool on a warm summer's day.

In the Gospel of John, Jesus shows the way to fullness of life, telling us that anyone who has faith in him will do the works he did - and greater works besides. The Risen One continues the dance of divine creativity in us who journey together, sisters and brothers with all living things on the way to the new creation where heaven and earth will be completely one - new and glorious with Spirit Creator as it was in the beginning, is in the process now, and will be forever to endless ages. We glimpse this vision, as in a glass darkly even now, as we strive to live in harmony with God's creation affirming, as God did at the birth of creation, that all things are good.

Jesus challenged us to greater works in the gospel. At the dawning of the 21st century, we are at the brink of undreamed-of possibilities to explore other planets and probe the new visions of the Mystery of Life. What does all this mean? Does it involve a fresh understanding of matter, energy, spirit and life? Are we called to be prophets and mystics? Now, more than ever it is time to put on our dancing shoes!

Shared Dialogue:
The community shares their thoughts on the theme.

Intercessions:

Let us dance together the dance of becoming with God. That we may care for the cosmos in which the Holy One is revealed, we pray to you our Creator...
(**Response** is: Lead us, O God!)

That those in leadership in our church may let go of fear of the new and wholeheartedly join in the dance, we pray to you, our Creator...

That theologians may have courage to respond to the rhythm of truth in spite of condemnation, we pray to you, our Creator...

That the dead may dance forever in God's presence, we pray...

(Other Intentions)

Presentation of Bread and Wine:

(Hold up bread and wine) Blessed are you, God of all life, through your goodness we have bread, wine, all creation, and our own lives to offer. Through this sacred meal may we become your new creation.

Eucharistic Prayer
Part One:

God of amazing surprises, Creator of tiny bugs and awesome planets, Designer of earth's wonders, Giver of life and laughter, we praise your passionate love hidden, yet revealed, everywhere in the cosmos.

We thank you that from the beginning, you called us to partnership with all creation in the holy dance that is all of life in your Divine Presence.
We praise you as we jump for joy in an explosion of grace that resounds through the universe.

All: Holy, Holy, Holy, God of dance and song, heaven and earth are robed in your glory. Hosanna in the Highest. Blessed are You who dwell among us. Happy are we who are called to this banquet of unending joy. Hosanna in the Highest.

Part Two:
We thank you for the women and men through the ages who have danced Love's cosmic dream of communion with hearts ablaze. We pause now to remember those who have shown us how to step lightly on the path to holiness. (Time for spontaneous remembrance)

We praise you, Christ, who calls us to deep intimacy in this Eucharistic celebration. We offer thanks for this gift, the Bread of Life and the Cup of Salvation, that will heal our hearts and transform our lives.

Part Three:
Before Jesus freely gave his life for us, he took bread, gave thanks, broke the bread, gave it to his friends and said:

All: Take this all of you, and eat it. This is my body which will be given up for you.

At the end of the meal, Jesus took a cup of wine, gave you thanks and praise, gave the cup to his friends and said:

All: Take this, all of you, and drink from it. This is the cup of my blood, the blood of the new and everlasting covenant. It will be shed for you and for all so that creation may reconciled. Every time you do this, remember me.

Let us proclaim the mystery of faith:

Christ, in your dying and rising, all creation leaps together toward a new earth and new heavens. Although we come from diverse backgrounds, we are one body, for we all share in this one bread. And so, as we join with one another in the cosmic dance, Creator God, we celebrate your holy presence in every living thing.

Let us live as a new body, brought to birth by the Spirit of the Risen One in acts of forgiveness, healing, and justice. Let us support all who suffer and work for peace in lands torn by violence and hatred.

All: Through Christ, with Christ, in Christ, in the resurrecting power of Divine Love, all glory and praise is yours, O Gracious God, forever.

The Prayer of Jesus: (Traditional or see appendix)

Breaking of Bread:
(Hold up bread and wine) Let us share the Body of Christ with the Body of Christ!

Communion:
Meditation Hymn: "In the Name of God" from John Michael Talbot's cassette *"The God of Life"*

Prayer after Communion:
Cosmic Christ, you have lifted us up and swung us around to see your beauty in nature's awesome gifts everywhere and in everyone. May we continue to move together to the divine rhythm of harmony and peace, dancing joyfully in love with all created beings forever.

Final Blessing of Community:
May we go forth as dancing prophets and mystic visionaries of our cosmic communion with all life, in the Name of the Creator, in the Name of the Healer, in the name of the Spirit. Amen

Closing Song:
"Come To The Circle Of Life" by Kathy Sherman on *"Faces of The Children"* or "Dancing Sophia's Circle" by Colleen Fulmer from cassette *"Dancing Sophia's Circle"*- Loretto Spirituality Network, 725 Calhoun St., Albany, CA 94756 Tel: 510-525-4174

Liturgy of Fire

(Easter Season, Pentecost, Earth Day, Social Justice)

Introduction of Theme:
O Holy One of burning bushes, enflame us with your passion for life, for justice, for creativity, for renewal, for play. Shekinah, appearing in the symbols of cloud, light and fire, you accompanied the Hebrew people through the wilderness. Travel with us through our desert and lend us a glimpse of your powerful feminine presence among us. Divine Compassionate Love, be our source of strength in our commitment to justice and peace. Dwell within us always as an eternal flame that will glow forever.

Opening Song:
"We're Coming Home" by Carolyn McDade or "You, God, are my Firmament" by Miriam Therese Winter, published by Medical Mission Sisters, or "Come Thou From Whom All Blessings Flow" by Jann Aldredge-Clanton, published by Twenty-Third Publications 800-321-0411 or "Come Holy Spirit" or "Veni Sancte Spiritus" from Taize on *Laudate* tape.

Greeting of Peace:
Let us reach out in love to one another.

Opening Prayer:
Shekinah, you show us the sacredness of Earth and all her creatures. You reveal yourself in wind, fire, and earth. May we celebrate with burning hearts the warmth of your passionate love in the outpouring of your miracles everywhere. May we join with others in works of justice and peace for our world.

Readings:
Pentecost: Joel 3:1-5, Romans 8:22-27

Women at Pentecost: Acts 1:12-14 or Acts 2:1-18
Shekinah: Exodus 29:45-46 or Exodus 25:8
Gospel: John 7:37-39, Matthew 9:17, Luke 1:46-56 or Luke 24:13-35

Homily:

Where is the passion in your life? Is the Pentecost-Fire stirring in you?
Has Shekinah whispered anything in your ear lately? What makes your heart
burn within you?

I see and hear the Spirit "a'movin'" all over the place. I glimpse her
presence in the feminine awakening in which women from different religions
and traditions are voicing their truth, claiming their inner authority, turning
away from patriarchal values and embracing their spiritual experiences.

Another place I discover her impact is in the re-emergence of feminine
divine imagery in creative rituals and traditional worship. As I use these
images in my prayer, I am discovering a new dimension of myself. For the
first time in my life I see myself as a powerful reflection of God's feminine
face. Gender equality is now more than a head trip for me. It is at the heart
of the transformation of patriarchy. It is the vision of Jesus and it will change
everything.

The scripture readings speak to us of Spirit-Fire spreading through the
cosmos, recreating Earth, renewing human hearts and transforming the
church. The same Spirit-Fire nudges people of our age to dream new
dreams of a world where there is no more discrimination, and inspires visions
of justice, equality and peace. Shekinah continues her whisperings through
contemporary prophets, like Dorothy Day who, with her vision of
nonviolence and pacifism, shakes people up. Indeed, Shekinah seems to be
doing a lot of shaking up today.   Many structures and institutions seem to be
falling apart.

Excitement, fear, doubt and confusion abound. A paradigm shift appears on
the horizon. Where are you?   Is the Spirit an ill wind shaking you up or like
a gentle mother comforting you? Or both? Is Shekinah guiding you over the

rugged mountains and low valleys of your struggles with life's ambiguities? Where are we as a faith community in our journey toward the fullness of justice? Will the church be renewed? It looks like we are back where we started, full of questions, full of wonder at Spirit Presence dwelling among us. Let' s take some time to share the "miracles" of Pentecost-Fire, the whispering of Shekinah in your life.

Shared Dialogue: The community shares their thoughts on the theme.

Intercessions:
Let us pray that Spirit-Fire may light up our world and renew all hearts. (**Response** is:Yes, Shekinah!)

That we may realize that creation is Shekinah's sanctuary, we pray...

That each of us may experience ourselves as Shekinah's dwelling place, we pray...

That the Spirit may transform all unjust structures in church and society, we pray...

(Other Intentions)

Presentation of Bread and Wine:
(Hold up bread and wine) Blessed are you, God of all life, through your goodness we have bread, wine, all creation, and our own lives to offer. Through this sacred meal may we become your new creation.

The Eucharistic Prayer:
Part One:
O Divine Flame of Love, your glowing embers dance in our hearts. Your passionate presence kindles our souls. You purify us with the searing truth that ignites our spirits. As the glowing embers of a fire penetrate the cold around us, so your tenderness sets our hearts aglow. We celebrate your nearness this day as we remember your Pentecost miracles.

How often have you loved us tenderly, without limits or boundaries! How often have you forgiven us freely and healed our sicknesses! How often have we been consumed with delight by human touch!

How often have you embraced us through Earth's beauty! How often have you affirmed us as your beloved creation! How often have you energized us to keep on keeping on - working for justice and peace in our world! We praise and exalt you forever with grateful hearts as we pray:

All: Holy, Holy, Holy, Fire of Love, heaven and earth burn with love for you.   Blessed are you who come to show us the depths of your yearning for us.   Hosanna in the highest.

Part Two:
Passionate God, kindle your fire of enthusiasm within us. Speak to us with assurance and excitement. Reveal to us the infinite, boundless, depths of your love for us. Awaken us to your promises to be always present in our lives, no matter what the obstacles or setbacks we experience. Consume us with such a hunger and thirst for justice that our words and actions may inflame others to become signs of your justice. Give us eyes to see human need, hearts to care for our sisters and brothers and hands and feet to lighten others' burdens.

Part Three:
Shekinah, we thank you for sending Jesus, your strong, but gentle presence, to bless and transform our lives. Jesus came to pour forth the love from your heart on all of us and show us how to live as your new creation.

The night before Jesus died, he gave us a special gift of love divine. He took bread, broke it and shared it with friends who gathered around the table saying:

All: Take this all of you and eat it; this is my body which will kindle your passion for God and for all God's creatures.

Then Jesus took a cup of wine, praised God, shared the cup saying:

All: Take this all of you and drink from it; this is the cup of my blood, the blood that will energize you with Spirit love; it will be poured out as kindling for the transformation of all.

Let us proclaim the mystery of wonder in our midst: Christ is the spark of love in whom we believe; Christ is the passion of God in whom we trust; Christ will be always the desire who consumes us. As we celebrate this memory of Jesus, let us pray that we, like the disciples on the road to Emmaus, will burn with love for the God of Surprises who breaks the bread of life and pours the cup of salvation over all creation.

Part Four:
May our hearts be merry on our journey as we dream new dreams and see new visions.   May we recognize Christ present in every person everywhere: all of us the Body of Christ - broken and shared. Every day as we care for each other, may we encounter the God who dwells with us anew. May we become Spirit-Fire, as we fan the flames of love over the entire cosmos.

Shekinah, be with our families and friends, the young and old, the sick and dying and all those who need your nurturing love this day. Reconcile all those who experience the pain of discrimination in our church. Bless, protect, heal, encourage, comfort each person and group we remember today: (Pause and name people you want to remember.)

As you led the Israelites through the bleak terrain, guide all those who are on their way home to you. (Pause and name people who have died whom you want to remember.)

Open us to Spirit-Fire igniting the Earth. May all creation dance in your presence. May we become one heart, one mind, one spirit with everything. May we touch the earth with reverent awe and live in harmony with all creatures. May we turn away from all efforts to dominate anyone or anything. May we see your face shining in the stars and in the sun. May we embrace the universe's treasures and celebrate life's simple pleasures each day. May your love kindle our friendship with all life. O Heart of Love, we dwell as one in you.

All: Through Christ, with Christ, in Christ the love of God is poured out into the whole world through the power of the Holy Spirit forever and ever. Amen.

The Prayer of Jesus: (Traditional or see appendix)

Breaking of Bread:
(Hold up bread and wine) Let us share the Body of Christ with the Body of Christ! Amen.

Communion:
Sing the "Eight-fold Alleluia" then make up own verses or "Glory to Thee O God of Life" by John Michael Talbot from *The God of Life* or "Veni Sancte Spiritus" from Taize or "You Are the Song" by Miriam Therese Winter from Medical Mission Sisters.

Prayer after Communion:
Thank you for this holy meal that we have shared. Fuel our hearts with your divine energy that we may share your love with all creatures. May we live always as instruments of your faithful love. Amen.

Final Blessing of Community:
May the fire of God's love ignite our hearts in love; may the passion of God radiate through us; may the Spirit of truth and justice burn within us forever. Amen.

Closing Song:
"One by One" by Miriam Therese Winter from Medical Mission Sisters or "We Give Thanks to You, Dear Earth" by Jann Aldredge-Clanton, published by Twenty-Third 800-321-0411 or "Thanks to Thee" by John Michael Talbot from *The God of Life*.

Liturgy for All Saints' and/or All Souls' Day

Introduction of Theme:
God wears all of Creation like a garment. Departed loved ones are like jewels in this robe that is Creation or like stars in the dark night sky of infinite Space. The saints, our saints, whether known to all or completely unknown, are the reflected glory of God.

Opening Song: "For All The Saints" or "God of The Gathering" by Kathy Sherman on cassette "*Faces of The Children*" - Sisters of St. Joseph of LaGrange, 1515 W. Ogden Ave., LaGrange, IL 60526-1721

Opening Prayer:
Today we rejoice in the holy women and men of every time and place. May they remain with us in prayer and love and memory and continue to guide this earth in God's evolving plan. Amen.

Greeting of Peace:
In communion with all our saints, living or dead, let us celebrate our oneness as we greet one another.

Readings: 1 John 3:1-3   Matthew 5:1-12

Homily:
Many of you may have seen the movie *Amistad*. If you did, you may remember the line, near the end, when the main character speaks of all his ancestors and says "Right now I am their whole reason for existing!" This may sound like a brash statement, but have you ever thought about it like that? Have you ever considered that you are the culmination of all of life's evolution in your family tree until now?

God is building a Body on earth. We have, in the past, called it the Body of Christ or the Communion of Saints. But it is truly an experience for God of dwelling in a biological reality. Each new division of cells into a brand new foetus is another step in the emergence of the divinity into form. We build physically on the DNA that we inherited from others and we build spiritually, as well, on the state of awareness that illumines the entire society from which we are spawned. Physically, emotionally and spiritually we are living on the building-blocks of past builders.

If we look at it like that, how must we thank the ones who nourished their bodies, minds and souls carefully to contain the emerging God who does and will dwell among us? How can we ourselves contribute to this living bank of God-seed that will continue after our death? I would like to hear your thoughts about this idea!

Shared Dialogue: The community shares their thoughts on the theme.

Intercessions:

That we may awaken to the needs of God's saints, especially those who experience rejection, alienation, injustice and poverty, we pray...
(**Response** is: Hear us, O God!)

That we may celebrate the Divine Presence in our relationships, especially in those closest to us, we pray...

That the sick may be healed, especially (mention names), we pray...

That the dead may dwell forever in God's presence, we pray...

(Other Intentions)

Presentation of Gifts:

(A small book has been prepared with the names of departed loved ones, mentors, special people whose memories we cherish. Each community member has had an opportunity to write names in the book. This is now brought forward and placed on the altar, along with the bread and wine, while all present call to mind those written in the book and ask for their presence with us here today.

Blessed are you, God of all Life. Through your goodness we have all these gifts: bread, wine and these precious lives to offer along with our own lives, the fruit of many lifetimes and work of many hands, present here today as the fruit of this earth.

The Eucharistic Prayer:
Part One:
We thank you, our God, that throughout history you have called to the human family and instructed us to love one another and to learn, from the humblest parts of creation, your hidden ways. May the saintly women and men of old, the cloud of witnesses who have gone before us, accompany us on our journey.

As we wait with joyful hearts for the fulfillment of your plan in our lives, we remember the prophets, martyrs, saints and mystics who have gone before us: Deborah, Isaiah, Mary of Magdala, Peter, Martha, Phoebe, Lydia, Irene, Patrick, Brigit of Kildare, Francis of Assisi, Hildegarde of Bingen, Catherine of Siena, Ignatius Loyola, Teresa of Avila, John of the Cross and all those we remember as heros and heroines in our church who inspire us today.

(Community names, mentors whom they want to remember, living and dead. This list is only partial. Each community needs to create their own according to custom and culture.)

Part Two:
As we share this holy meal, we remember the holy men and women who drank from Wisdom's well and showed us how to live as courageous disciples: the prophet Miriam, King Solomon, the woman at the well, Paul of Tarsus, Prisca and Aquila, Clare and Francis of Assisi, Dorothy Day, Jean Donovan, Dorothy Kazel, Ita Ford, Maura Clark, Oscar Romero and all those companions we cherish and who bless and challenge us on our faith journey.

All: Holy, holy, holy, God of sinners and of saints, Lover of weakness and of strength, wisdom of the heavens and of this gentle earth, blessed are we to whom you are made known!

We honor the ones who have revealed your ways to us until we could
recognize them for ourselves. We thank you for the courage and fidelity of
all the ones you sent to prepare a path for us to follow - the holy women and
men of every age and culture.

Part Three:
We especially thank you for Jesus, who came to us as bread for our
journey. He has become Living Bread and we seek to follow his example:
we, the Body of Christ, feeding the Body of Christ to the Body of Christ in all
our interactions and relationships. In Christ you revealed the complete
mystery of love that is the human family.

On the night before Jesus gave up his life, he took bread into his hands and
made clear the reason that you had sent him among us.

All: This is my body, he said. Take it and eat of it. Then continue to do
this to remember me.

At the end of the meal Jesus took a cup of wine, raised it in thanksgiving to
you, and said,

All: This is the new covenant of my blood which I shed for you and for all,
so that creation may be reconciled again. Every time you do this, do it to
remember me.

Now then, let us proclaim the mystery of our faith:
In every creature that has ever breathed, Christ has lived;
in every living being that has passed on before us, Christ has died;
in everything yet to be, Christ will come again!
In our breaking of the bread of earth, Christ is being re-membered!

Part Four:
O Holy One who lives in our hearts, we celebrate your radiant image in men
and women everywhere. Your creativity flows through our beings. Your joy
fills us. Your blessings are the wellspring of grace all around us. Your mercy

is fresh, like dew, every morning. Your healing liberates us from all darkness and oppression. Your empowerment bubbles up inside us. For you are the Love that dwells in our depths, the Wisdom of the Ages that speaks through us, the Divine Connection that makes us all one. Amen.

All: Through Christ, with Christ, in Christ the love of God is poured out into the whole world through the power of the Holy Spirit forever and ever. Amen.

The Prayer of Jesus: (Traditional or see appendix)

Breaking of Bread:
(Hold up bread and wine) Let us share the Body of Christ with the Body of Christ! Happy are we and all who have gone before us to become part of the Cosmic Sacrifice of Love.

Communion:
"Break open The Bread Of Your Life" by the Monks of Weston Priory or "I Am The Bread Of Life" or "The Brighter Side" by Michael Rowland

Prayer after Communion:
Holy One, we praise your glory reflected in our fellowship of saints. May we who share at this table be filled with your love and made ready for the joy of your communion with all the saints. Amen.

Final Blessing of Community: May the God of Sarah and Abraham bless you; may the God of Jesus and Mary Magdalene bless you; may the God of your mothers and fathers bless you and may you always find the fellowship of the saints.

Closing Song:
"When the Saints Go Marching In"

Fall Liturgy Honoring Julian of Norwich

(Appropriate for any season of year)

Introduction of Theme:
> (Altar or table has been adorned with simple things from nature - fall leaves, fruit, wheat, any appropriate and simple items.) Our theme today honors the writings of Julian of Norwich. She was a young woman who lived in England during the 14th century. She had many mystical visions which stressed the goodness of God's creation and of its creatures. That is why we chose her today. Julian was also a linguist. She was able to communicate in new ways what she felt God was trying to show of the mystery of God's Love. She was an anchoress and she took the name of the patron saint of the church to which she attached herself. No one knows her real name. (Tell more of her story, if desired.)

Opening Song: "For The Beauty Of The Earth" or "Touch The Earth" by Kathy Sherman on "*Faces of The Children*" - Sisters of St. Joseph of LaGrange, 1515 W. Ogden Ave., LaGrange, IL 60526-1721 Tel:708-354-9200

Greeting of Peace:
> God, we ask you to grant us an insight of the unity of our being, as we greet one another with the peace that was given to us by the Christ in our midst.

Opening Prayer:
> In the name of the Creator of the universe and of the Redeemer sent among us and of the Spirit of Holy Sophia, we come together to celebrate our moment upon this planet.

> God, our Creator, open our eyes to see your hand at work in the splendor of creation and in the beauty of human life. Open our eyes further to see our own hands at work as co-creators with yours. Touched by your hands, our world is holy. Help us to cherish the gifts of people like our sister, Julian and

the gifts of one another as we experience the joy of being a community of co-creators.

1st Reading: (from *Praying with Julian of Norwich* by Ritamary Bradley, p.139)
Then our Lord opened my spiritual eye and showed me my soul in the center of my heart. I saw the soul as extensive as if it were an *endless world* and a *blessed kingdom.* And from the kind of place it was, I understood that it is a *glorious city...*

When the soul comes above all creatures into the self, it cannot stay there, beholding that self. Rather, all of its beholding is directed blissfully to God --that God who is the maker, dwelling therein.
for in the soul of humanity is God's true dwelling place.
And the supreme light and the brightest shining of that city is the glorious love of the Lord, as I see it.

2nd Reading: (from *Praying with Julian of Norwich* , p.166 & p.143)
Our Lord showed himself many times reigning, but principally in the human soul.
--There is his place of rest and his noble city.
--From this noble see he will not go forth nor remove himself -- ever.
--Marvelous and awe-inspiring is the place where our Lord dwells.
He wants us, therefore, *to give our attention* to his gracious touching:
--more enjoying in his holy love
--than sorrowing in our frequent failings. (p.166)

For God loves us and takes delight in us, [saying]: "I want you to love me, to delight in me, and fully to *trust* me." *And all shall be well.* (p.143)

3rd Reading:
Philippians: 2:6-11

Homily:
The reading from Philippians reflects the mission of Christ in its cosmic dimension, as he was sent from God to perfect and free human and all

nature. Jesus himself tells us that we live in God and God lives in us. We are icons of God, reflections of divinity in our world.

In Philippians, we are asked to bend the knee to this profound and startling revelation about nature itself! Our own nature contains the indwelling divinity as revealed in the person of Jesus.

Carl Jung assures us that our true Self is nothing less than the image of God that has been imprinted in our own unique soul and which is the "king" or ruling entity of our being. If we align ourselves with our eternal purpose we align ourselves with the will of God for us. The Christ-center of each of us is fully intact and glorious.

Shared Dialogue: The community shares their thoughts on the theme

Intercessions:
"Here is God's supreme courtesy: that we are invited to become part of the good that is done. ..
--the *good* God wishes to do in our lives and in the lives of others -- in those who sorrow, in those in prison, in those who prosper, in those in positions of power.
--the *good* God desires to do to do in the times in which we live...
Let us pray that these things be done." (Bradley, p. 104)

That we may cherish the gifts of creation all around us each day in the air we breathe and in all creatures, great and small, we pray to you, our Creator...
(**Response** is: God, hear our prayer!)

That we may use our artistic and poetic talents, Julian did, to praise God and all of nature, we pray to you, our Creator...

(Other Intentions)

Presentation of Bread and Wine:
(Hold up bread and wine) Blessed are you, God of all life, through your

goodness we have bread, wine, all creation, and our own lives to offer.
Through this sacred meal may we become your new creation.

Eucharistic Prayer:
Part One:
Great and holy designer of all that is, from everlasting you are God! You
have woven the fabric of the universe and spread it before you as the dwelling
tent of your glory. You have invited all creation to robe itself in the love
poured out from your heart as from a fountain of never-ending abundance.

We thank you for the extravagance of your giving, for the endless communion
of your presence among us in all that is. We thank you that throughout
history you have called to the human family and instructed us to love one
another and to learn from the humblest parts of creation your hidden ways.

All: Holy, holy, holy, God of darkness and of light, wisdom of the heavens
and of this gentle earth, you who come to us as matter and as spirit; blessed
are we to whom you are made known!

Part Two:
We honor the ones who have revealed your ways to us until we could
recognize them for ourselves. We thank you for the courage and fidelity of
all the ones you sent to prepare a path for us to follow - the holy women and
men of every age and culture. We especially thank you for the Christ, who
came to us as bread for our journey. He has become Living Bread and we
seek to follow his example: we, the Body of Christ, feeding the Body of
Christ to the Body of Christ in all our interactions and relationships. In him
you revealed the complete mystery of love that is the human family.

Part Three:
On the night before he gave up his life, Jesus took bread into his hands and
made clear the reason that you had sent him among us.

All: This is my body, he said. Take it and eat of it. Then continue to do
this to remember me.

All: At the end of the meal Jesus took a cup of wine, raised it in thanksgiving to you, and said, This is the new covenant of my blood which I shed for you and all, so that creation may be reconciled again. Every time you do this, do it to remember me.

Now then, let us proclaim the mystery of our faith: In every creature that has ever breathed, Christ has lived; in every living being that has passed on before us, Christ has died; in everything yet to be, Christ will come again! In our breaking of the bread of earth, Christ is being re-membered!

Part Four:
And so, as we take our places in this moment on the stage of human history, O God, send your gracious Spirit upon us again. Help us to recognize the reality of Christ present and risen from death among us. Let us take courage and find power to exult in our great mystery as people on a journey. Teach us to live gently and gratefully upon this planet and upon the pathway you have chosen for us from among the stars.

Breaking of Bread:
Break bread; then elevate bread and wine while saying: "I am the sovereign goodness of all things. I am what makes you love...This I am -- the endless fulfilling of all desires." **(words are Julian's)**

Let us share the Body of Christ with the Body of Christ! Amen.

Communion:
"Mother Divine" by Kurt Van Sickle, ISUN Music, P.O. Box 141217, Austin, TX 78714

Prayer after Communion:
Creator of all, you have revealed the beauty of your nature through the beauty of our world. May this creative power of your love be in our hearts to bring your joy to all we meet. We ask this through the Cosmic Christ. Amen.

Final Blessing of Community:
That all may be well, and that all may be well, and that all manner of things
may be well with you in the name of the God who creates, the God who
redeems, the God who makes us whole and holy.

Closing Song:
"Blessing Song" by Miriam Therese Winters, Medical Mission Sisters or
"Send Us Forth" by Kathy Sherman on *Faces of The Children*"

Wedding Liturgy

Processional:

Both sets of parents could be in the processional as a symbol of the power of two individuals, the Bride and Groom, coming from different rich heritages and choosing to join their traditions together in a new family.

Introduction of Theme:

We come together to celebrate the joining of (name Bride and Groom) in holy matrimony. We pray that their love may be the fulfillment of the covenant, given to us by a God who is boundless, passionate love, the perfect manifestation of forgiveness, tenderness, intimacy and playfulness. We rejoice with (name Bride and Groom) in this celebration of their sacred commitment.

Greeting of Peace:

Let us express our friendship and support of (name Bride and Groom) as we share a sign of peace with one another.

Opening Prayer:

God of lovers, hear our prayers for (name Bride and Groom) . They bring before you their hopes and dreams as they join their lives together in a union of hearts so intimate that it is the most perfect human symbol of your divine love for humankind.

Readings: Genesis 1:26-27; 1 Corinthians 13; John 15:9-16

Homily:

Today, our homily is preached by the witness of (name Bride and Groom), who pledge their love and fidelity in their marriage commitment. By their love for one another, they are reflecting love's power, God's passionate, tender presence revealed in intimate human relationships. Their future is an act of faith, with all its promises and challenges, hopes and dreams. Today they stand before us , and risk everything in walking this path together through good and bad times, no matter what happens. They are saying "yes", they believe in one another, they hope in one another, they love one another.

Let us pledge our support and friendship to them in the days and years ahead. (Name Bride and Groom), we promise to be there for you in your successes and failures. We promise to love you in your joys and sorrows, triumphs and sufferings. You are a visible sign to us that true love calls us to care for one another, and that relationships, even in our disposable society, are worth the hard work it takes to maintain them.

(Name Bride and Groom), your vowed commitment reminds us that love is a treasure worth pursuing with our hearts and that Lover God is present every time we reach out to touch another person with smiles, caresses, open hearts and listening ears. Today your wedding reminds us of our call to reach out to others with compassion. You challenge us to believe that love can work miracles and that we can be channels of Lover God's healing, empowering love in the world. Amazing Grace, how much more love you give us , than we can ever hope for or imagine!   Let us immerse ourselves in God's infinite love and become, like (name Bride and Groom), the face of God for each other.

(Name Bride and Groom), we celebrate with you this day and pray that you will grow more deeply in love with one another in Lover God's passionate heart. May your commitment to fidelity be a source of hope for all of us this day that love can always be new and fresh, like a summer breeze; that love can grow and grow, like the seed that is transformed into the tallest of trees; that love is forever striving for new heights and depths of intimacy, like the human hearts who seek love's fullness again and again. Thank you for preaching to us today! We bless you! We love you!

We now invite your family members to share their words of encouragement and love as you begin your wedded love this day.

Declaration of Intent:

(Name Bride and Groom), you have come together to witness your faith in one another as you pledge your love. The God of Lovers embraces and blesses you as you hold one another this day in mutual love. Since it is your desire to enter into this sacred relationship, join your hands and proclaim your love before God and this community.

(Name Groom), do you take (name Bride) to be your loving, equal partner for as long as you may live? (I do.)

(Name Bride), do you take (name Groom) to be your loving, equal partner for as long as you may live? (I do.)

Exchange of Vows:
(It is recommended that Bride and Groom create their own marriage vows that reflect their loving commitment. The following is an adapted version of the traditional vows.)

(Name Groom), repeat after me. I, (Groom), take you, (Bride), to be my lover, friend, and companion as long as I may live. I promise to be faithful to you in happy and sad times, in sickness and in health. I will cherish and love you as my beloved forever.

(Name Bride), repeat after me. I, (Bride), take you, (Groom), to be my lover, friend, and companion as long as I may live. I promise to be faithful to you in happy and sad times, in sickness and in health. I will cherish and love you as my beloved forever.

Blessing and Exchange of Rings:
(Name Bride and Groom), you will now symbolize your eternal love through the giving and receiving of rings. The circle of a ring symbolizes a love that lasts forever. May these rings remind you of your passionate love for one another, a love that will endure the tribulations of life, a love that will grow stronger with each passing day. May the bliss of romantic love that you now experience be a mere shadow of the happiness that lies ahead in your married life.

Faithful God, bless these rings that (name Bride and Groom) may experience overflowing love for one another in your abiding presence everyday of their lives.

Presider gives groom the bride's ring:
(Name Groom), place this ring on (name Bride's) finger and repeat after me: (name Bride), I give this ring to you as a sign of my faithful love. I will love you all the days of my life.

Presider gives bride the groom's ring.
(Name Bride), place this ring on (name Groom's) finger and repeat after me: (name Groom), I give this ring to you as a sign of my faithful love. I will love you all the days of my life.

(Name Bride and Groom), you have promised to give yourselves in self-giving love to one another in the exchange of these rings. Now I declare you blessed forever and joined together as husband and wife. You may now kiss one another.

Unity Candle (Optional)
The two candles represent your individual lives, families, cultures, and backgrounds. As you light the Unity Candle, you symbolize the powerful union you now share as a married couple bringing these two traditions together in a new family.

Intercessions:
As (name Bride and Groom) are united in this holy union today, may they be signs of your intimate love calling us to open, caring relationships with one another..
(**Response**: God of lovers, unite us in love.)

That all God's creatures may experience justice, peace and harmony, we pray...

That we, the people of God, may reflect harmony and peace in all our relationships, we pray...

That (name Bride and Groom) may be dynamic witnesses of your passionate tender love for all people, we pray...

That we, the friends and relatives of (name Bride and Groom), may be blessed with all we need to grow spiritually as a family of faith , we pray...

. That our deceased loved ones, especially those we remember today, may experience God's eternal embrace. (Let us pause now to name our loved ones.) And for all the dead, we pray...

That God may answer the special prayers we bring today, we pray... (Time for spontaneous petitions from community.)

Presentation of Gifts:
(Instrumental and /or classical music may be played as family members bring gifts to altar.)
(Hold up bread and wine) Blessed are you, God of all life, through your goodness we have bread, wine, all creation, and our own lives to offer. Through this sacred meal may we become your new creation.

The Eucharistic Prayer:
Part One:
God of passionate love, Initiator of romantic desire, Spirit of union, we delight in your playful tenderness and intimate communion revealed in married love. We thank you that from the beginning, you called woman and man to equal partnership in the sacred bond of holy matrimony. We praise you as we celebrate the mystery of divine love that is reflected in the union of (name Bride and Groom), whom you have joined in marriage this day.

All: Holy, Holy, Holy, God of lovers. Heaven and earth are bound together in your eternal embrace. Hosanna in the Highest! Blessed are you who call us to loving relationships. Happy are we who are called to this wedding feast of boundless joy. Hosannah in the Highest!

Part Two:
We thank you for (name Bride and Groom). May their marital union be a
sacred experience of your healing, forgiving, empowering love. We praise
you for married couples whose love has illuminated our lives and flooded our
hearts with brilliant insight into the presence of the holy all around us.

We express our gratitude to you, Lover of all Lovers, who call us to
undreamed of closeness with you and all God's people in this sacred meal.
We are one body, your body. We offer thanks for this holy bread and wine,
signs of our communion with you and with the entire cosmos, that we will
share around this festive table.

Before Jesus freely gave his life for us, he took bread, gave thanks, broke the
bread, and shared it with all those at the meal saying:

All: Take this all of you and eat it. This is my body which will be given up
for you.

At the end of the meal Jesus took a cup of wine, blessed you, Lover of all
Lovers, shared the cup with all those at the meal saying:

All: Take this all of you and drink from it; this is the cup of my blood, the
blood of the new and everlasting covenant; it will be shed for you, and for all.

All: Let us proclaim the Love of the Ages: Christ, by your cross and
resurrection, we are set free from all fear and negativity to soar to love's
heights in your presence.

Part Three:
We are a family of faith bonded together in joy as we celebrate our union in
this holy meal. May the married love of (name Bride and Groom) flourish
and be a beacon of light for all the world to see.

 Let us pray for the earth in which your divine indwelling is manifested.
(Mention nature's gifts which we cherish.)

Part Four:
Let us pray for all people around the globe, especially the poor, the oppressed, the neglected, the "least" of our sisters and brothers. (Mention specific intentions.)

May we let go of all that keeps us from caring for one another with sincere hearts.

All: And so we pray: through, with and in our Lover God, in the unity of the passionate Spirit, we give glory and praise to you, Love of the Ages, forever and ever. Amen.

The Prayer of Jesus: (Traditional or see appendix)

Breaking of Bread:
Let us share the Body of Christ with the Body of Christ! Amen.

Communion:
"Wherever You Go" by the Western Priory Monks

Prayer after Communion:
O Everlasting Love, you draw us closer together in your divine embrace. May you hold (name Bride and Groom) close to your heart forever, as you delight in their sacred union. We ask this through Christ, our companion in life's journey. Amen.

Final Blessing of Community:
Family and friends of (name Bride and Groom), let us raise our hands in blessing for this newly married couple: God of Love, bless (name Bride and Groom) with joy and peace on this their wedding day. May their home be a sacred place of welcome for all who dwell there. May they grow more deeply in love every day of their lives. May their love be fruitful and may they give you glory and praise, one in mind, body and spirit forever.

Closing Song: (See attached sheet)

Appendix One

Alternative and Contemporary Versions of the Prayer of Jesus

1. Divine Parent, you are everywhere; sacred is your presence.
    May your family grow in oneness and closeness to you,
    as we forgive ourselves, others, and you for the hurts that wound us.
    Show us how to love as you love. Help us to embrace one another as family.
    Empower us to meet every challenge. Deliver us from all that divides us,
    for you are our Mother/Father, the Giver of Life forever and ever. Amen.

2. Our God, who brought us into being and dwells in all creation,
    Holy is your name.
    May your new creation come; may your heart's desires be fulfilled.
    Nourish us this day with all that we need.
    Forgive us our failures and heal our brokenness
    and give us, too, forgiving hearts.
    Strengthen us to resist temptation; deliver us from evil.
    For yours is the power and glory that dwells everywhere in the cosmos,
    forever and ever. Amen.

3. Our Birther God who dwells among us, we praise your holy name.
    Your love be born in us; Your will be done. You give us all we need.
    You forgive us and help us to forgive others.
    You deliver us from evil and liberate us to live in freedom.
    For you are the Creator, the Lover and the Empowerer that enfolds us forever
    in your Divine Womb-Love. Amen.

4. O God of Love, You dwell everywhere.
    Holy is your passionate presence everywhere and in everyone.
    Your vision be praised; Your dreams be fulfilled in us and in all generations.

You give us all we need to be free and whole.
You forgive us our failures and heal the wounds of our souls.
Your reign will be forever glorious. Amen.

5.   O Passionate God of Love, You dwell in the hearts of all people.
Intimate Warmth is your Name. May your tenderness be felt!
Embrace us this day in your compassionate arms.
Forgive us our failures to love and heal the hurts of our hearts
and give us the power to heal one another.
Help us to let go of resentment and all that separates us from one another.
Deliver us from hostility.
For Yours is the brilliant beauty and magnificent power of Divine Love
forever. Amen.

Appendix Two

Music Suggestions for Weddings

Processions:

Wedding March 111by Ernest Bloch
Cantilena by Joseph Rheinberger

Hymns:

Come To The Circle Of Life - by Kathy Sherman - Ministry of the Arts, 1515 W. Ogden Ave.,
LaGrange Park, IL 60826-1721 Tel: 708-354-9200
Come and Sing Praises - *Praise Six* by Maranatha Singers
Joyful, Joyful, We Adore Thee
Glory and Praise To Our God - *Glory and Praise*
Love Divine, All Loves Excelling
How Great Thou Art
Amazing Grace
On Eagle's Wings - *Glory and Praise Vol. 2* - 10802 N. 23rd Ave., Phoenix, AZ 85029

Solos:

Wherever You Go
Ave Maria
O Perfect Love
Make Us One
Take Our Lives
Wedding Song by Henry Schultz - *Song of Ruth*
Like A River Glorious
Be Thou My Vision
That All May Be One by the Monks of Western Priory
I Have Loved You by Michael Jorcas, *On Eagle's Wings*
Rachel's Song from *The Instrumental Album* composed by David M. Combs

Books Cited:

Bradley, Ritamary. 1995. *Praying with Julian of Norwich*. Mystic: Twenty-Third Publications.

Cooke, Bernard.1997. *The Future Of Eucharist*. New York: Paulist Press.

Durkin Dierks, Sheila. 1997. *WomenEucharist*. Boulder: WovenWord Press.

Schaeffer, Pamela. *National Catholic Reporter*. January 9, 1998.

About The Authors:

Mary Beben is a presider for a small faith community in Burke, Virginia and serves as a spiritual director and counselor. She is currently studying full-time for her degree in psychology and women's spirituality. She counts among her greatest blessings her 41 year marriage to her husband, Joseph, with whom she has raised six children and with whom she has also traveled the world in the service of the U.S. Military. She has spent her life studying theology and spirituality and developing methods to help awaken the people of God to their full inheritance of God's kingdom/queendom among us.

Bridget Mary Meehan, a Sister for Christian Community (SFCC) holds a doctorate in ministry from Virginia Theological Seminary and a Master of Arts degree in spirituality from the Catholic University of America. She is a spiritual director, conference speaker, retreat director, workshop leader and consultant in women's spirituality in Europe and the United States. She is the author of fifteen books, including *The Healing Power of Prayer* (Liguori Publications), *Exploring The Feminine Face Of God, Delighting In The Feminine Divine,* (National Catholic Reporter), *Heart Talks With Mother God,* (Liturgical Press), *Heart Talks With Mother God,* and *Praying With Women Of The Bible,* (Liguori Triumph). She is a producer and host of *Godtalk,* a new cable TV program that aims to nurture the soul, heal the heart, expand consciousness, transform lives, and inspire believers of all faiths. Dr. Meehan offers a visionary approach to wholeness and healing for women and men as disciples of Jesus and equals in the contemporary world. She also coordinates a Women Eucharist group in Northern Virginia.

Both of the authors are certified members of the Federation of Christian Ministries and are authorized to witness marriages, preside at liturgies, proclaim the gospel and function as ministers of the Christian Church.

They are available, separately or together, to facilitate the emergence of small faith groups as they begin to take steps toward egalitarian and reverent liturgies. They may be consulted for retreats , workshops, and private spiritual direction.